Magnificent Monterey and the Big Sur Area

First edition
Copyright © 1989 Maxine Knox and Mary Rodriguez

Published by Lexikos

Edited by Laurie Cohn

Typeset and Designed by Louisa Shopes and The Mac Studio, San Francisco, CA for DCIF Press

Set in 12 pt. Goudy. Reproduced from pages generated on a Macintosh SE computer and printed on the QMS 810 Laser printer.

Cover by Janet Wood

Cover Photo by Kent Reno

Fonts supplied by Software for Le$$, San Francisco, CA.

ISBN 0-938530-41-0

Printed in the United States of America

CONTENTS

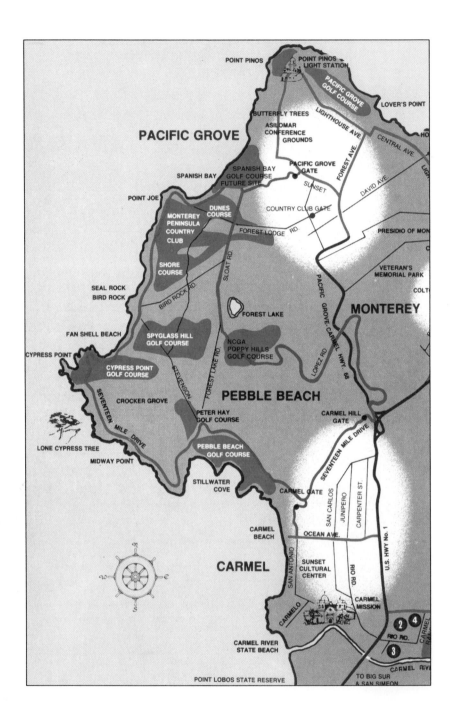

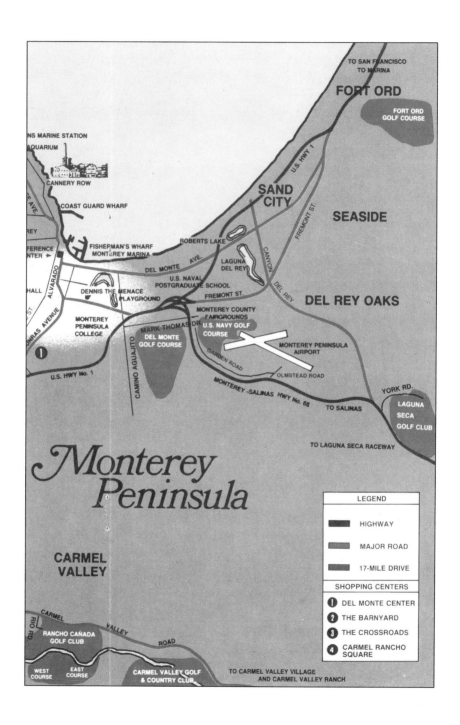

Directory of Pictures

INTRODUCTION

The Monterey Peninsula/Big Sur area has a special magic all its own. Rocky coastline, white sandy beaches, primeval forests, mist-shrouded mountains, crisp, smog-free air, and an artistic and historic atmosphere will make you want to return again and again. Each time you will discover something new and different to do and see. You can enjoy a restful holiday or a visit crammed with challenging activities and adventures because there is something for everyone of every age and every interest.

Jutting out into the Pacific, the Monterey Peninsula is framed by the rolling ocean on two sides and the lulling waters of Monterey Bay on the other, with the forest greenery and majestic mountains of Big Sur completing the canvas. Located on the Central California Coast, it is 125 miles south of San Francisco and 345 miles north of Los Angeles and is easily accessible by car, bus, or plane. Running through the Monterey Peninsula and connecting with major highways to the north, south, and east is California's first designated Scenic Highway, Highway 1 through Big Sur country. Interstate buses, an intracity bus service and charter bus, limousine, and helicopter tours are provided. Several scheduled airlines service the Peninsula, and private plane facilities are excellent.

The climate is pleasantly temperate. In winter months, when rainy days alternate with sun-filled weeks, the average temperature is fifty-seven degrees, and in summer, sixty-seven degrees. Morning and evening fog cool the coastline but disappear by midmorning. It is never really cold and seldom hot, nearly always sweater weather. You can golf, fish, or play tennis during any month. Casual clothes are acceptable almost everywhere.

Because the Monterey Peninsula is so attractive to visitors and a popular choice for large conferences and small group meetings, it is well to plan ahead so you won't be confronted by "no vacancy" signs. This is particularly true in summer months and during the time of special annual events, such as, the Pebble Beach National Pro-Am Golf Tournament, Laguna Seca Races, the Monterey Wine Festival, or the Monterey Jazz Festival. For an uncrowded holiday, consider the fall and winter months when some motels have lower rates, and check the Calendar of Annual Events in the last chapter of this book. If you decide to attend one of these exciting happenings, reserve your tickets, if needed, and your accommodations well ahead of time.

The Monterey Peninsula is made up of several individualized communities: Pacific Grove, Pebble Beach, Carmel, Carmel Valley, Del Rey Oaks, Sand City, Seaside, Fort Ord, and Marina. Though of divergent origins, they complement each other and merge into a delightful area different from anywhere you have ever been.

By taking you along a simple route, this book will help you discover the special magic of the magnificent Monterey Peninsula and Big Sur country on your own.

CHAPTER ONE

MONTEREY, THE OLD AND THE NEW

Monterey's existence and fortunes have been tied to the bay that shares its name since Juan Rodriguez Cabrillo, a Portuguese navigator in the service of Spain, first sighted it in 1542. Cabrillo noted this body of water in the ship's log but did not land on the tree-lined shore. The first visitor was Basque explorer Sebastian Vizcaíno who named the area "Monterey" in honor of his sponsor, the Count of Monterrey, and took possession of it in the name of Philip III of Spain. Vizcaíno strongly recommended that the area be colonized as an outpost of the Spanish empire, but King Philip ignored him. It wasn't until nearly two centuries later, on a June morning in 1770, that Captain Gaspar de Portolá, Governor of Baja California, came by land with a small band of Spaniards, and Padre Junipero Serra, a Franciscan monk, arrived by sea. They met on the beach, raised a flag and claimed the area once again for Spain. Padre Serra set up the second Alta California Mission, while Captain Portolá established the Presidio. Thus, the settlement of Monterey began with the cross and the sword as its symbols.

The Mission was later re-established at its present location in Carmel because Padre Serra wanted to remove his Indian neophytes to a quieter, more spiritual setting away from the sometimes rowdy Spanish soldiers in Monterey. The original Mission, the present-day San Carlos Cathedral, was known as the Royal Presidio Chapel and served the soldiers attached to the Presidio.

At first Monterey was only a fort. Five years after the founding of the Presidio, soldiers' families settled and Monterey became a pueblo. With game plentiful, the forest thick with timber, the land fertile, water abundant, and temperatures moderate, the colony could not help but prosper. When Mexico obtained independence from Spain in 1821, Monterey served under a second flag as the capitol of Alta California at various times between 1775 and 1846. The town was incorporated in 1850.

Monterey's geographical location makes it the hub of the Monterey Peninsula. Today it is a city of twenty-seven thousand, deliberately uncommercial and with an aura of gentility which has led it to shun any form of air-polluting industry. Revenue is derived from the Peninsula's military installations, from institutions of higher learning, from a series of annual events, and the scenic, artistic, and historic atmosphere which makes Monterey attractive to travelers.

Live-oak-lined Highway 1 (Cabrillo Highway) leads into the Monterey Peninsula. When approaching Monterey, take the Fremont Street entrance. If you are coming from the north, stay in the right lane: there is a tricky spot where the left lane suddenly branches off without much warning, by-passes Monterey, and goes south to Carmel.

Points of interest turn up immediately as you enter the city on Fremont Street. **Santa Catalina School,** in the woods to the left off Mark Thomas Drive, is a Catholic co-educational day school, pre-school through eighth grade, and an all-girls boarding and day school from grades nine through twelve. The main building is an excellent example of Spanish-Colonial architecture revived. Though built in 1929 as a private residence, the methods employed were the same as those of early artisans who used no modern tools. Whitewashed stone slab walls, a red tiled roof, and an abundance of wrought iron detailing make it reminiscent of early Monterey haciendas.

On the right of the highway is the **Naval Postgraduate School.** Here selected officers of the Navy, Marine Corps,

Old Del Monte Hotel, now the Naval Postgraduate School

Army, Air Force, and Coast Guard, as well as officers from allied countries, are educated for leadership in the world of technology, science, and management. The handsome old buildings with their tailored grounds, strolling peacocks, and swan lake were once part of the most deluxe resort on the West Coast and, even now, are often referred to as "the old Del Monte Hotel." It was opened in 1880 by the redoubtable four San Francisco multimillionaires: Leland Stanford, Mark Hopkins, Collis P. Huntington, and Charles Crocker. The elite of San Francisco and Southern California arrived in their private cars at the hotel's own railroad station, but Del Monte Hotel never quite lifted Monterey to the social eminence enjoyed by Newport and Saratoga on the Eastern seaboard. A modest museum in the basement of Herrman Hall (site of the old hotel) is a repository for significant mementos relating to the building's history.

When World War II created a dearth of help and patrons, the hotel was leased to the U.S. Navy in 1940 as a preflight training center. This famous old resort was closed as a hostelry in 1951 when the Government bought it and surrounding acreage as the location of the newly expanded Naval Postgraduate School. The buildings have been converted into administration offices, classrooms, and living quarters for bachelor and foreign students. All enjoy the elegant Roman plunge, tennis courts, and acres of well-tended gardens where, in the early 1900s, millionaires and their ladies mingled with a new kind of West Coast society.

A left turn at Aguajito Road will lead to **Old Del Monte Golf Course** (public). Follow the directional signs to the oldest golf course west of the Mississippi, built in 1896 as part of Del Monte Hotel's guest facilities. The first tournament was held the following year and was so successful that it became an annual event which developed into the California State Amateur Championship.

Overlooking the intersection of Fremont and Aguajito on the tree-clad hillside is **Monterey Peninsula College.** This is a two-year, tuition-free community college.

A right turn off Fremont at Camino El Estero will take you along willow-fringed **Lake El Estero.** Pedal boats and canoes can be rented on the far side of the lake. On the shore across the bridge is a shady picnic area with tables and grills. A pleasant walking and jogging path encircles the lake. The parcourse is a quarter-mile trail stopping at eighteen numbered fitness stations. It starts near the ballpark between the two estuaries.

A curving row of eighteen huge polished boulders of rare California black granite grace the shore park of the other branch of the lake at Fremont and Camino El Estero. This art form by Lloyd Hamrol was commissioned by the City of Monterey.

Dennis the Menace Playground, designed by Hank Ketcham, Dennis' creator, and built by the Monterey Peninsula

4

Junior Chamber of Commerce, is also at Lake El Estero. This is a certain stop if you have children along. Its landmark is a real, stationary Southern Pacific steam locomotive for scrambling over and pretend-engineering. There are several wading pools, a swimming pool, unusual swings, slides, tunnels, and imaginative mazes, all free to enjoy.

The **Visitors and Information Center** is in the Armed Forces Y.M.C.A. building at the corner of Webster and Camino El Estero and is open every day from 9 a.m.- 4:30 p.m. Here you can pick up free brochures and a guide to Monterey's Path of History, a self-guided tour of forty-six historic sites, which will make your visit even more pleasurable. An inexpensive street map of Peninsula cities would be a wise investment.

The **First Presidio**, older than the United States, was built by Costanoan Indian laborers on the site behind the Y.M.C.A. building. In recent years archaeologists have uncovered its adobe foundations, and the fenced diggings have brought up many military and Indian artifacts.

Returning to Fremont Street will facilitate sightseeing. Turn right on Church Street. In the next block you will see the original Mission founded by Padre Serra, now **San Carlos Cathedral.** This Registered National Historical Landmark is open to the public. Though small, it is a typical example of Spanish-Colonial architecture embellished with splendid Mexican folk art. This was the first Presidio Chapel, the most important church politically and religiously in California in the early 1800s. Building plans were drawn up by the Academy of San Carlos in Mexico City and are still on file in Mexico's National Archives. The **Royal Presidio Chapel** was completed in 1794 under the direction of Padre Fermin de Lasuen and the Mexican master stonemason, Manuel Ruiz, with the help of Indian workers. Ruiz also directed construction of the Carmel Mission. The Chapel was enlarged in 1858 when Monterey was a whaling port; sections of whale vertebrae were used to pave the front sidewalks. The picturesque bell tower was added in

1893. In constant use since 1794, the church did not deteriorate as did other Missions when they were abandoned after the devastating secularization of the Missions in 1834. At that time many of the furnishings from the old Carmel Mission were brought to San Carlos Church. In 1850, when the Diocese of Monterey included all of California, the Royal Presidio Chapel became a Cathedral. Later the diocese was divided and the Chapel lost its high standing, but in 1968 it became a Cathedral once more.

An interesting sidelight about San Carlos Cathedral is that Lou Henry and Herbert Hoover were married by a Catholic priest in the front courtyard on February 10, 1899. Both young people were Quakers, but since there was no Friends meeting-house in the vicinity, Miss Henry's father, a prominent local banker, arranged with the Bishop for a civil ceremony at San Carlos.

Behind the Cathedral is the trunk of the famous, old oak tree under which Mass was said when Vizcaíno landed in Monterey in 1602. Padre Serra, recognizing the site from Vizcaíno's description, offered Mass for the Portolá expedition under the same tree. Though badly damaged by lightning in 1840, the **Junipero Oak** still gave forth new shoots. When a utility company chopped it down and threw it in the bay in 1905, the dismayed chaplain had local fishermen retrieve it and place it in its present position.

Visitors who wish to see Monterey's historic sites will find directions on twelve signs showing large maps of the downtown area with historic landmarks indicated. The redwood-framed signs, 32" x 40", have been put up at Custom House and at Custom House garages, at Portola Plaza, at the Pelican Monument area, at Fisherman's Wharf parking lot, at the end of Alvarado Mall near the lower plaza, at the park by Stevenson House, at Pacific House annex, at Scott and Pacific Streets, and at Cooper-Molera Adobe.

You can sense more of Monterey's fascinating past by meandering along the **Path of History.** Following the big blue dots

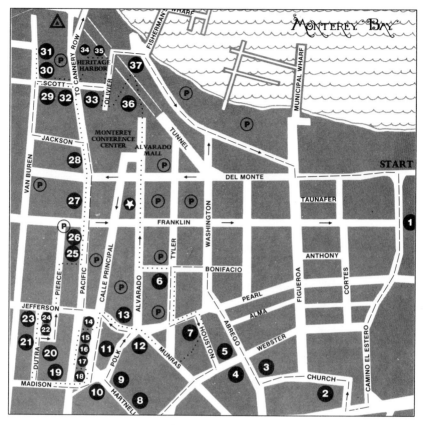

Monterey's fascinating Path of History

painted on sidewalks will take you to the most important sites in this cradle of California history. Some are private offices and residences, but many are open to the public; a few have gift or antique shops and restaurants. These authentically restored buildings are a credit to the members of the Monterey History and Art Association, who saved most of the original homes from destruction and meticulously renovated them in conjunction with the State of California Department of Parks and Recreation. Each spring the Association hosts an Adobe House Tour. Hostesses dressed in Spanish-Colonial costumes serve as guides. Free maps for this self–guided tour along the Path of History are available at the Monterey History and Art Association office in Casa Serrano, 412 Pacific Street (open Saturday and Sunday from 2-4 p.m.), or at 550 Calle Principal at Custom House Plaza (open Monday through Friday from 9:30 a.m.-12 p.m. and 1-4 p.m.). You can begin your walk at any location on the map.

There is a distinctive building design called "the Monterey style," a reminder of Spanish and Mexican times, plus a little Johnny-come-lately influence. The term "adobe" refers to a house built of mud mixed with straw, which retained heat in winter and kept the sun's rays from penetrating in the summer. Whitewash (lime) was applied to the outside walls to form a sort of plaster. Land was cheap; a typical house was built with plenty of space around it, usually in the center of a courtyard, and constructed crosswise to the compass, letting the sun shine for some part of each day into every room. The house had two stories, and a balcony extended halfway or all the way around the upper story. In the Spanish-Mexican period, stairs to the bedrooms were usually outside. Although it is said this encouraged elopements, such a design had its practical aspects. The returning master could clean up without tracking dirt through the ground floor rooms, and he could also sneak in and out unsuspected if circumstances necessitated. New England influence later placed the stairs on the inside.

Some early Yankee settlers were ships' carpenters who built their homes of pine and redwood, so plentiful in the area. Dirt and tiled floors were replaced with wood, and shutters were put on the outside rather than inside. The custom of building outside doors in pairs, with each single door too small for a person to pass through, was continued. There was wisdom in this since it was a good protective device. Eventually, the practical New Englanders replaced Monterey's bougainvillea-draped adobe walls and tile copings with white picket fences.

Many interesting Path of History sites are clustered in and around downtown Monterey. One is **Stevenson House** on Houston Street, which was owned by Jules Simoneau. Robert

Louis Stevenson rented a room here in the autumn of 1879 while courting his future wife, Fanny Van de Grift Osbourne, ten years his senior and the divorced mother of two children. She was visiting her sister and escaping from her unhappy first marriage. Stevenson House, now a State Historical Landmark, is an outstanding example of an adobe dwelling. Its rooms are filled with accurate furnishings and bric-a-brac of the nineteenth century as well as the largest collection of Stevenson memorabilia in the United States. Youngsters will be fascinated by the Simoneau children's room because it is filled with small-sized period clothing and antique toys. The house in intriguing, also, because it has an alleged ghost or two. Sometimes the shadowy, romantic figure of Robert Louis Stevenson himself has been seen standing at the top of the stairway. Tours of Stevenson House are conducted daily, except Wednesday, at 10 and 11 a.m. and at 1, 2, 3, and 4 p.m.

Pleasant **Jules Simoneau Plaza** with fountains, flowers, benches, and town clock is at the corner of Tyler and Munras. Not only was Simoneau Stevenson's landlord, but he was an encouraging friend who provided the destitute young writer with free meals at his restaurant and saloon which stood on this spot. This is also the Monterey Peninsula Transit Plaza.

Across the street is the completely restored **Cooper-Molera Adobe** complex, the largest in Monterey's State Historic Park, covering two-and-one-half acres. Within its charming rural confines are the Cooper Colonial House with some of the original furnishings, Diaz Adobe, the Corner Store, Spear Warehouse, a kitchen garden, chickens in their coop, and two barns. The Corner Store faces Polk Street; some of the sundries popular in the mid-1800s are sold here. The complex is open Wednesday and Saturday, noon-5 p.m., with tours at 2, 3, and 4 p.m. The Corner Store is open Wednesday and Saturday from 10 a.m.- 4 p.m. Cooper-Molera Adobe was built in 1830 by Captain John Rogers Cooper who arrived in Monterey in 1823.

Children's Room. Stevenson House

Munras Avenue leads into Alvarado Street (one-way west), Monterey's downtown business district. The pretty, brick-paved, tree-bordered semi-mall at the west end of Alvarado Street leads to the **Monterey Conference Center** and Custom House Plaza. The main offices of the **Monterey Peninsula Chamber of Commerce** and its **Visitors and Convention Bureau,** which serve the entire Peninsula, are in Rodriquez-Osio Adobe, 380 Alvarado. Chamber hours are 8:30 a.m.- 5 p.m. Monday-Friday in winter, and also on Saturdays, May through September.

Monterey's Conference Center has a 20,000 square foot exhibition hall, an 11,000 square foot ballroom, a 500 seat forum, and additional small meeting rooms. In addition to being a convention facility, the Center is used for social and cultural events.

A 6'7", 1,400 pound bronze statue of Don Gaspar de Portolá proudly surveys **Portola Plaza** at the Conference Center. This Bicentennial gift from Juan Carlos I was created in the Spanish Province of Lerida, Portolá's birthplace. Coincidentally, this is how a nearby street happened to be named after the King of Spain.

A 9' x 45' ceramic tile mural interpreting the rich history of the Monterey Peninsula is an eye-appealing point of interest on the outside wall of the Monterey Conference Center facing Pacific Street. Its focal point is an early Spanish sailing vessel much like the ones that brought various explorers to the shores of Monterey. The artist is Guillermo Wagner Granizo.

Larkin House, the first recorded two-story adobe in Monterey, built in 1835, is at the intersection of Munras and Jefferson. This building served as the American Consulate in Alta California when Thomas O. Larkin was U.S. Consul at the Port of Monterey. The parlor is considered one of the one hundred most beautiful rooms in America. Larkin House is open from 10 a.m.-5 p.m., closed Tuesdays.

Across from Larkin House is **Friendly Plaza,** a delightfully old-fashioned brick courtyard planted with trees, shrubs, and flowers from all over the world. Particularly notable is the **Moon Tree,** a redwood. The seed from which it germinated was carried on the January 1971 Apollo Flight 14 by Major Stuart Roodon.

Monterey's famous landmark, **Colton Hall,** dominates the area between Jefferson and Madison on Pacific Street. In its day it was the most pretentious building in California and still is one of the state's most distinguished edifices. Colton Hall was constructed with soft, yellow-white sedimentary rock called "chalk rock" or "Carmel stone," which came from a quarry just outside of town. This rock was also used for most of the foundations of adobe homes and for garden walls. Walter Colton, first *alcalde* (mayor) of Monterey, was responsible for the first newspaper published in the state, the first school, and the first library. He

One of the one hundred most beautiful rooms in America,
the Larkin House Dining Room

came here as a Congregational chaplain aboard Commodore
Sloat's frigate *Congress* and stayed on to govern the citizenry.
There is an excellent free museum on the second floor of Colton
Hall, open daily from 10 a.m.-noon and 1-4 p.m., and until 5
p.m. in spring and summer.

Monterey Peninsula Museum of Art, across the street, is
fully accredited with the American Association of Museums and
has a prestigious permanent collection of art, including a room
of folk art upstairs. There is also a book and gift shop. The
yearly calendar of events includes selective one-man shows,
exhibits, slide shows, lectures, and art classes. Admittance to
the museum is free. Hours are 10 a.m.-4 p.m. Tuesday through
Friday, and 1-4 p.m. Saturday and Sunday, closed holidays.

Two blocks up the hill at 440 Van Buren Street is the **Monterey Institute of Foreign Studies.** Some of the classrooms are

housed in the old Carnegie Library, the first in Monterey. The Institute is an independent, fully accredited, upper division and graduate school with a predominantly foreign-born and foreign-educated faculty. This is the only educational facility in the country completely committed to preparing students for positions as foreign service officers for the State Department, for work in the foreign service of other countries, and for preparing them in areas like multi-national corporate management.

Perry House, a charming Victorian with a spectacular view of Monterey Bay, is at the corner of Van Buren and Scott Streets. Manuel Perry, a whaling captain, built this home in 1860.

Mayor Hayes O'Donnell Library, in the middle of the next block on Van Buren, was Monterey's first Protestant church. This century-old chapel was originally built on Pacific Street by the congregation of St. James Episcopal Church. When urban renewal threatened, the Monterey History and Art Association intervened and saved it by having the building moved to this site. It may surprise you to see a red church.

Oldtime melodrama endures

Protestants painted their churches white in New England, but Californians always preferred red for their classic, little Gothic churches. The library's collection is concentrated on Californiana. The mellowed wooden floors are covered with Oriental scatter rugs. The period furnishings fit with their setting; display cases hold antique buttons and fans, old quilts, and other cherished items from Monterey's early days. The library is open Wednesdays and Saturdays from 1-4 p.m.

California's First Theatre, a museum by day and a theatre by night, is a block down Scott Street at the corner of Pacific. In the middle of the nineteenth century, this was a saloon and sailors' boardinghouse operated by Jack Swan, after whom the little restaurant here is named. In 1847, a small group of soldiers from the Presidio volunteered to present two minstrel shows, and Swan's tavern became the first building on the Pacific Coast in which paid dramatic performances were staged. Now the Gold Coast Troupers present live, old-time melodramas Wednesday through Sunday evenings in the summer, and Fridays and Saturdays during the winter. The box office is open summer afternoons so you can reserve tickets. Sip "sassparilla," hiss the villain, and cheer the hero. It's all-around good family entertainment.

The long, two-story adobe down Scott Street with the characteristic balcony on four sides is **Pacific House,** a former hotel and saloon for seafarers. The house and grounds cover one-third of a city block. There was a bull-and-bear pit here during Spanish and Mexican days; today it is **Memory Garden** where Monterey celebrates her birthday with a *Merienda* (fiesta) each June. The lower floor of the house is a public museum of Monterey lore, open 10 a.m -4 p.m. daily. Of special interest is the Costume Gallery. The collection numbers around three thousand items dating from the nineteenth century to the 1950s.

The **Old Whaling Station** on short Decatur Street nearby was built as a private residence in 1885 and later became a boardinghouse for a group of Portuguese whalers. These men formed the Monterey Whaling Company and devised improved methods for harpooning humpback and California grey whales. Vessels totaling 640 moved between the California coast and the Hawaiian Islands. Some of the harpooners were South Sea natives with painted bodies and scanty, colorful dress who shocked local residents with their partial nudity. Whalebone fences were common, and the sidewalk in front of the Old Whaling Station is made from whalebones, as is the mantle over the entrance to California's First Theatre. The price of whale oil declined, and whalebone use was limited; by 1877 the Pacific Coast whaling fleet was reduced to forty ships. Since 1937 grey whales have been protected by international agreement. They still ply their passage along the coast on annual trips to Mexican waters in winter, returning north along the same route in spring. The Junior League of the Monterey Peninsula restored the Old

Old Whaling Station

Whaling Station and has offices here. Docents conduct tours every Friday from 10 a.m. to 2 p.m.

In **Custom House Plaza** you can wander through expanses of red-roofed, white adobes surrounded by seasonal flowers. Plane trees provide shade and a Spanish fountain a lyrical note. Adjacent to the plaza is a bocci (pronounced bott-chee) ball court where retired Sicilian fishermen play their national game which resembles outdoor bowling.

Close by Custom House, near the entrance to Fisherman's Wharf, is a handsome bust of Pietro Ferrante, one of the three pioneers who founded Monterey's fishing and canning industry. Ferrante was awarded the Italian Congressional Star for the generous assistance he gave to other Italian immigrants who settled in this country.

The Old Custom House

Custom House was built by the Mexican Government in 1814 and is the oldest government building west of the Rockies. This is where, in 1846 during the war with Mexico, Commodore John Drake Sloat raised the American flag, claiming all of Alta California for the United States. This famous adobe has exhibits from three periods of California's history when Monterey was the capitol. Four flags fly over the Plaza: Spanish, Mexican, American, and California's Bear Flag. Many special events are held here, including the re-enactment of Sloat's Landing each July.

Allen Knight Maritime Museum, next to Custom House Plaza, reflects Monterey's nautical past. This museum was named after a former mayor of Carmel who collected many of its exhibits. Admission is free. Hours are 1-4 p.m. weekdays and 2-4 p.m. Saturdays and Sundays; closed Mondays and holidays. *Turkey*, a twenty-six foot boat built in 1915, stands alongside the Museum and has been designated a historical commercial fishing vessel.

The entrance to **Fisherman's Wharf** is next to the Custom House. Summer days and sunny weekends you will be greeted by the organ grinder and his affectionate monkey. Much of the activity on this pier centers around the wholesale and retail fish business. Two of the markets have been operating since the 1930s. Tourist attractions on the wharf are geared to family fun. Sandwiched between fish markets, boat sales, rentals, and excursion concessions are restaurants, gift shops, bazaars, art galleries, and candy shops. The many-colored buildings perched on old pilings have a certain charm. Graceful gulls circle overhead, and pampered sea lions bark and beg from the waters below. Most of the restaurants on this wharf serve sand dabs, squid, and abalone, all local delicacies.

The new **Wharf Theatre** was built from the same plans as the former one which burned many years ago. Several well-known actors advanced their thespian careers in the old theater, including the late Richard Boone.

Monterey's Fishing Fleet at dawn

Glass Bottom Belle, a motorized glass-bottomed boat operates from 11 a.m. to 6 p.m. on holidays and weekends, and daily during summer months from Rappa's Seafood Grill at the end of the wharf.

Municipal Wharf No. 2 is to the east beyond the parking lots. This pier was built in 1926 to accommodate larger ships coming into the harbor. It is the working wharf with wholesale fish warehouses at the end. You can watch commercial boats unload squid, tuna, sole, salmon, cod, kingfish, anchovies, and herring, while squawking gulls taunting fishermen as they clean their catches. Monterey is one of the leading squid ports in the United States, exporting hundreds of tons annually to Europe and the Philippines.

If you would like to do some drop-line fishing for tom cod or sunfish, bait is free with rod rentals on both wharves. You can launch your own boat from Wharf No. 2. The **Monterey Peninsula Yacht Club** and its marina filled with bouncing craft is here, too.

Monterey Municipal Beach, east of Wharf No. 2, is a sandy, mile-long stretch. The warm, shallow water in this spot is good wading for small children. The whole beach is good for sunbathing and picnicking. Open fires are not allowed, but you may use a camp stove or hibachi.

At the entrance to the tunnel leading to the Presidio is a typical, small, double-ended fishing boat, the *Santa Maria.* Three generations fished from its decks. The monument notes the contribution of pioneer Sicilians to Monterey's fishing industry.

Follow the shoreline west to the **Presidio of Monterey** overlooking the harbor where dozens of fishing boats are moored. The Presidio was moved from its original level site near Lake El Estero in 1792 to these 409 hillside acres which command a dramatic view of Monterey Bay. While driving through the Presidio, be sure to observe the strictly enforced traffic

The little fishing boat that supported three generations of Sicilian families

regulations; this is a military reservation. Most of the streets at the Presidio were named after distinguished members of the 11th Cavalry stationed here during the early 1920s. However, Sgt. Beans, who had a road named after him, was a mongrel smuggled into the post to become the Cavalry's beloved mascot. The dog was even listed on the division's roster, and the entire 11th Cavalry stood at attention for Sgt. Beans' funeral.

Once reverberating with the sound of bugles, marching feet, and horses' hooves, today the Presidio is the **Defense Language Institute,** the largest language school in the free world. Training is provided in thirty-five languages, including many dialects in each. The enrollment represents all branches of the service. The instructors are, with few exceptions, natives of the countries whose languages they teach.

Another historic spot on the Monterey Peninsula is at the Pacific Street entrance to the Presidio. This ten foot monolith marks the approximate site of the Junipero Oak, which was moved to San Carlos Cathedral. An ornate cross, the profile of Padre Serra, and a bas-relief of San Carlos Cathedral are carved on the stone column. The boulder marker to the left commemorates Gaspar de Portolá's official claiming and colonization of Alta California for Spain in 1770.

The large granite eagle sculpture on the hillside memorializes Commodore John Drake Sloat's landing at Monterey in 1846. He came to annex Mexican Alta California, which included what is now California, Nevada, Arizona, Utah, and parts of New Mexico, Colorado, and Wyoming, to the United States.

On the bluff overlooking Fisherman's Wharf is another monument , a man and a boat ringed by a wrought iron fence. It was erected in 1891 to honor Padre Serra's landing in Monterey in 1770.

A tall wooden cross on the brow of the hill marks the site of a village of the Presidio's primordial inhabitants, the Rumsen Indians. Their settlement was an important one, judging from the large, pitted, nearly two thousand-year-old rain stone found in the area, a mark of distinction among Indian villages.

The Indian and military artifacts and photographs displayed in the **U.S. Army Museum,** below the eagle sculpture, trace the history of Presidio hill during Indian, Spanish, Mexican, and American occupation. The museum is open Monday through Friday from 9-11:45 a.m. and 12:30-4 p.m., closed holidays.

The above sites and others of importance can be seen by following the designated Historical Walk at the Presidio.

Follow the shoreline once again to one of the most celebrated streets in the world— **Cannery Row.** Until Nobel- and Pulitzer-prize-winning author John Steinbeck drew world-wide attention to it, the street was called "Ocean View Avenue." Steinbeck's novel *Cannery Row,* published in 1944, immortalized the oily setting and offbeat cast of characters who were actually a part of Monterey's booming sardine industry. This famed street also provided the setting for *Sweet Thursday.*

An inquisitive sea otter

After whale and sea otter hunting diminished, Monterey again looked to the bay for resource. In the 1940s the city became "the Sardine Capital of the Western Hemisphere, " adding a new mystique to Monterey's reputation and a colony of Sicilian fishermen to its population. In a peak year over two hundred thousand tons of sardines were processed in plants on Cannery Row. The silver fish filled the city's coffers with gold until the late forties when they mysteriously disappeared from the bay. There are many theories about this phenomenon, some based on fact perhaps, others pure fancy. No one really knows why they left. Monterey's economy sagged and personal fortunes were lost as cannery owners auctioned their plants and equipment, and fishermen mortgaged their homes to keep their boats. A small fishing fleet still chugs out of the harbor in the early mornings and brings back catches to be sold on Fisherman's Wharf and to restaurants throughout the Peninsula.

Old-timers who were not involved in the sardine industry are the first to tell you that they had no personal regrets about the sardines' departure. In Monterey's heyday when canneries worked round the clock, a malodor hung over the city for days at a time. Ladies held cologned handkerchiefs to their noses when going out. Cannery Row was certainly no tourist mecca in those days.

A hush fell over the Row as canneries folded, and Monterey suffered another shock to its economy. Monterey recovered; the street was reincarnated with the new and the old standing side by side, and Cannery Row became one of the major attractions of the Monterey Peninsula.

Cannery Row starts at the Coast Guard pier. Monterey's base has a ninety-five foot cutter. Two smaller boats, forty and forty-four feet, also work out of Monterey. The U.S. Coast Guard's primary mission in this area is "search and rescue."

The marina near the Coast Guard base is generally crowded with skindivers. They get in and out of their wet suits and inflate their brightly colored rafts next to their parked cars, which jam the vacant bayshore lots during daylight hours. Sea otters and sea lions entertain here, too, to the amusement of divers and a gallery of spectators.

In the middle of the nineteenth century, sea otters were hunted off the Central Coast for their desirable fur. This was an important economic factor to Monterey. The otter population in the Pacific once numbered two million, but by 1867 they had been hunted to near extinction. Fortunately, the sea otter has reappeared and has increased in numbers under government protection. Rafts of otters can be seen off Cannery Row, along the Pacific Grove, Pebble Beach and Big Sur shorelines, and at Point Lobos.

The author who immortalized Cannery Row

The most remarkable feature about the sea otter is that it is the only marine animal known to use a tool. Floating on his back , the otter places a large flat rock on his stomach, holds a shellfish, such as a mussel or turban snail, with both of his paws, and then brings it down hard on the rock to crack it. Surely there is no more cunning sight in local waters than that of a mother sea otter floating leisurely on her back in a kelp bed and cuddling her baby on her chest, looking like a wet teddy bear, while both are rocked by gentle off-shore waves.

Some dilapidated cannery buildings and warehouses, with their salt-stained, cracked windows and weather-worn names on their sides, stand idle. This is the way the disappearance of the sardines left them. Many oil-soaked canneries have been destroyed by fire. Others have been renovated and now house an assortment of businesses. You will be in the midst of a new and different Cannery Row lined with hotels, restaurants and cocktail lounges, art galleries, specialty shops, and antique stores. You will never go hungry or thirsty on Cannery Row. Some of the Peninsula's finest restaurants are here, and it is also the center for much of the area's night life.

The Monterey and Pacific Grove Railway Company operated between downtown Monterey and Pacific Grove until 1923. The clanging, thirty-five passenger Cannery Row trolley was patterned after it and offers a twenty-five minute narrated tour along the Row from 9 a.m.-9 p.m. daily. For one "Steinbuck" ($1) you can purchase an all-day ticket, getting on and off wherever and whenever you please. Tickets are available at the Cannery Row Historical Center garage, 275 Cannery Row, or from the conductor at eight designated stops. For $8 you can park in the garage all day and receive tickets for your whole party.

John Steinbeck wrote:

> Cannery Row in Monterey in California is a
> poem, a stink, a grating noise, a quality of light,
> a tone, a habit, a nostalgia, a dream. Cannery

Row is the gathered and scattered tin and iron
and rust and splintered wood, chipped pave-
ment and weedy lots and junk heaps, sardine
canneries of corrugated iron, honky tonks, restaurants and whore houses, and little crowded
groceries and flophouses.

His words are inscribed on the plaque of a bronze bust of
the author which stands under a cypress tree next to the sidewalk
on the shoreside of Cannery Row near Prescott.

Cannery Row has not changed so much that you cannot
imagine "Doc" Ricketts, a real life character and Steinbeck's
good friend, and his cronies reeling up the wooden stairs to his
brine-cured Pacific Biological Laboratory at 800 Cannery Row,
now a private club. Lee Chong's Heavenly Flower Grocery (Old
General Store) is across the street. Surprisingly, current day
Cannery Row characters are equally as colorful as Steinbeck's
fictional ones. Some businesses have adopted names from
Steinbeck's books to sustain the old Row atmosphere, but they
are not actual sites.

Once eighteen canneries worked night and day, serviced
by a fleet of one hundred fishing boats. More than four thousand
names were on the membership rolls of the Cannery Workers'
Union. Each plant had its particular whistle that blew to sum-
mon workers. They streamed on foot down the hill from New
Monterey or arrived by the cab-load. The last lone cannery
closed in 1973. If the sardines return en masse, no one will be
ready to welcome them.

Monterey Bay Aquarium at the west end of Cannery Row,
the largest indoor aquarium in the world, opened officially in
October 1984. The 177,000 sq. ft. building is located on the
site of the old Hovden cannery and incorporates part of the
original layout. Hovden, with its Portola brand, was the last
cannery to close on Cannery Row. Here in dramatic displays
of marine life are more than five thousand creatures representing

The Aquarium's Kelp Forest

nearly three hundred species and filling some twenty major habitat galleries and exhibits.

Several types of sharks, octopuses, chambered nautiluses, and various other open-ocean fish navigate the 90' long, 1/3 million gallon Monterey Bay Exhibit. California sea otters frolic in an innovative two-story exhibit, one of the most popular in the aquarium. The Kelp Forest Exhibit, the aquarium's center-piece, towers three stories.

Suspended from the ceiling are large-as-life models of marine mammals, including a forty-three foot gray whale and her calf. Some of the unusual exhibits include a bat ray touch pool and a touch tidepool where visitors can pick up starfish, a variety of crabs, and the like. There are also a walk-through, open-air shorebird aviary, a kelp lab, an indoor/outdoor coastal stream, a wave-crash exhibit, and an anchovy cylinder. Other attractions are slide and movie presentations, as well as numerous video, telescope, microscope, and magnifier displays for visitors to use. On the second floor is an art gallery with related changing presentations.

Part of the Aquarium's ongoing educational program is an outreach van called "Aquaravan" which has enriched the lives of thousands of school children with traveling marine exhibits. The Aquarium also supports a rehabilitation program, caring for stranded and injured marine mammals.

State-of-the-art technology has been the key to the construction of the Monterey Bay Aquarium and its exhibits, as might be expected. Members of the David Packard family (of Hewlett-Packard) have figured prominently in the planning of the Aquarium from the initial idea to its present status. The $40 million to build the Aquarium came as a gift from David and Lucile Packard. Once opened, the Aquarium has operated on a self-supporting, non-profit basis.

The Aquarium is open every day, except Christmas Day, from 10 a.m.-6 p.m. Tickets, available at the door, are $7 for adults; $5 for students and seniors, sixty-five and over, and $3 for children, ages three through twelve. To insure admission on holidays or during summer months, advance reservations may be made through Ticketron.

A free shuttle bus operates daily between downtown Monterey and the Monterey Bay Aquarium during summer months, and on weekends and holidays the rest of the year.

Three blocks up the hill from Cannery Row is a business and residential section called **New Monterey,** a name left over from other days. Actually it is one of the oldest parts of the city and sprang up during the sardine era. Fisherfolk and cannery workers lived on the hillside and some still do. Lighthouse Avenue is the main shopping district. Here you will find various businesses, including grocery stores, restaurants, antique shops, secondhand stores, and **Scholze Park** at Lighthouse and Hoffman with a children's playground.

CHAPTER TWO

PICTURESQUE PACIFIC GROVE

San Francisco Methodists had been seeking a suitable spot for a seaside Christian resort for some time, and they found it on this northernmost point of the Monterey Peninsula. Indian tribes from the inland vacationed in these groves of pines and oaks many years before and restocked their larders with mussels, abalone, and fish.

In 1875 a group of ministers from the Methodist Episcopal Church formed the Pacific Grove Retreat Association and put an almost indelible mark on the customs and laws of the city. Their policies and restrictions concerning immorality extended one mile in all directions from the center or town. Pacific Improvement Company (forerunner of Del Monte Properties Company, now Pebble Beach Company) was formed, and land was purchased from Southern Pacific and from David Jacks, a wealthy rancher. A tent city was laid out on 30' x 60' lots. Furnished tents, heated by wood stoves, rented from $2.25 to $5.50 a week. At the close of each summer season, the striped tents were carefully packed and stored in **Chautauqua Hall**, built in 1881 at Seventeenth and Central Avenue. It was restored recently and is used for many community events. In the early days of this century, Chautauqua sessions drew crowds from as far as San Francisco and Sacramento to hear sermons and lectures and enjoy uplifting entertainment. Chautauqua Hall, in addition to being used as a church, was also the site of Pacific Grove's first school in 1884.

The stockholders of Pacific Improvement Company generously agreed that they would donate a site for a church and parsonage to any religious organization that asked for property. Pacific Grove, as a Methodist retreat, held meetings outdoors or in tents. **St. Mary's-by-the-Sea Episcopal Church** was the first formal religious edifice to be built. Services have been held in this English Gothic building, at Twelfth and Central Avenue, since 1887. William H. Hamilton, a well-known Sacramento architect, patterned the original small chapel after one in Bath, England. It was 32' wide and 70' long, with a 75' spire. In order to enlarge the little church and add a chancel, sanctuary, and porch without marring its classic lines, it was sliced in two crosswise and three bays were added in the middle. The interior is finished in natural woods — walnut, pine, redwood, and cedar. Tiffany glass lancet windows with white lilies and pink foxgloves are of particular interest. Soon local carpenters were copying St. Mary's Gothic styling as they built homes in the area. Other buildings have since been added to the Episcopal church property to accommodate the growing congregation.

Idyllic Pacific Grove became a haven for other denominations, too: Catholics, Congregationalists, the Christian Church, and Salvation Army all established churches here before the turn of the century. In the early 1900s, the Christian Scientists, Baptists, and First Assembly of God built their churches.

Southern Pacific excursions from the San Francisco Bay area brought hundreds of people to Pacific Grove; the round trip cost one dollar. During summer months three or four eighteen-car trains ran along the waterfront and spilled their passengers so they could picnic on the beach, enjoy the seacoast, or attend Chautauqua events. Picnicking on the Sabbath was ruled illegal in Pacific Grove; so trains were discontinued on Sundays. By 1926 the Chautauqua era had ended.

The Methodists fenced their little compound, rang the curfew bell at 9 p.m., and locked the gates. There were rigid rules concerning dancing, drinking, and public bathing. Bathing suits had to be made of "opaque material, which shall be worn in such a manner as to preclude form. All such bathing suits shall be provided with double crotches or with skirts of ample size to cover the buttocks." A far cry from today's bikinis! Whatever laws weren't on the books were understood, anyway. While living in Monterey, Robert Louis Stevenson wrote of Pacific Grove: "Thither, in the warm season, crowds come to enjoy a life of teetotalism, religion, and flirtation, which I am willing to think blameless and agreeable.

Expenses for running the campground were paid by selling lots for $50 each. Eave-to-eave, board-and-bat cottages sprang up on former tent sites and can be seen along the narrow streets between Lover's Point and Pine Avenue. Year-round residents built handsome mansions. Within ten years Pacific Grove became the "Cultural Center of the West." The first Chautauqua (an assembly for educational purposes, combining lectures and entertainment) was held in a tent in June 1879 and later in the Old Chapel (Chautauqua Hall), now designated a California Registered Landmark. The city hosted three Presidents: Benjamin Harrison, William McKinley, and Theodore Roosevelt.

Pacific Grove was bounded by the beach on one side and by fences on the other three. The gate at the wagon and carriage entrance was kept padlocked. Peddlers and tradesmen from Monterey were forbidden to come in and sell their wares. In 1880 State Senator Benjamin Langford, who had a summer home nearby, grew tired of locking and unlocking the gate and took an ax to it. Thus Pacific Grove was dramatically freed from fenced-in isolation and joined the rest of the Monterey Peninsula. Fifty years later Dr. Julia Platt, a maiden-lady scientist and the city's first and only woman mayor, took an ax to another gate at Lovers Point and earned here nickname "Lady Watchdog." A Christian campground blossomed into a charming city and became incorporated in 1889 by its thirteen hundred permanent residents and was chartered in 1927. Pacific Grove's present population is eighteen thousand, and the city has grown to 2.6 square miles.

Provincial Pacific Grove has relaxed at last. For ninety-six years the sale of alcohol was prohibited except for medicinal purposes; pharmacists were kept pretty busy filling prescriptions! In spite of the continuing efforts of the small Pacific Grove Retreat Association to keep the town dry, in 1969 voters broke loose from this restriction and today liquor is sold in what was then California's last dry town.

Pacific Grove is known as **"Butterfly Town U.S.A."** and rightly so. For over one hundred years tens of thousands of bright orange and black monarch butterflies (*Anosia plexipus*) have migrated each October from the Northern Pacific states, British Columbia, and Southern Alaska to winter in the groves of trees, only to become restless and fly away to the north in March. This annual miracle is one of nature's mysteries and not yet scientifically explained because these monarchs have never been here before; each new generation senses the way to Pacific

Pacific Grove Royalty

Grove. The Pacific Grove Museum of Natural History, Forest and Central Avenues, has an exhibit showing the monarchs' migration pattern. The butterflies hang in huge clusters like dried leaves in the tall pines in Butterfly Trees Park on Lighthouse Avenue, at the Alder Street side of Washington Park and in scattered trees throughout the city. On sunny days what you might think is a dead tree will suddenly come alive in a burst of flaming color which slowly disseminates into lazy, velvet-winged butterflies fluttering over town gardens. Leave your net at home! The maximum penalty for molesting a monarch butterfly in Pacific Grove is a $500 fine and a six-month jail sentence! Hundreds of costumed school children herald the return of the monarchs every October by marching in the Butterfly Parade, followed by the Butterfly Bazaar. Gordon Newell's granite sculpture of a monarch stands in Lover's Point Park, one of few monuments in the country honoring the insect world.

David Avenue is the dividing line between Monterey and Pacific Grove. Drive to the west end of Cannery Row, turn left, then right, and you will be on Ocean View Boulevard and ready to peruse picturesque Pacific Grove.

Thousands and thousands of oval sardine cans were manufactured at the American Can Company on your left when Monterey was "The Sardine Capitol of the Western Hemisphere." Now it is called **American Tin Cannery** and is filled with outlet shops.

A mile-long section of the **Monterey Peninsula Recreational Trail** begins across from American Tin Cannery next to the Monterey Bay Aquarium and goes along Pacific Grove's shoreline. This is an eight-foot wide, asphalt-paved path for walking, jogging, or bicycling.

On the shoreside is **Monterey Boat Works.** Many of the fishing boats working out of Monterey during the sardine era were built here, and some are still in service. Now owned by Stanford University, the building has been renovated inside to

Where many sardine fishing boats were built

provide enlarged facilities for **Hopkins Marine Station** on China Point just ahead. The exterior has been restored to its original state. Hopkins Marine Station is an educational and research facility specializing in the study of intertidal life. It was the first marine laboratory on the Pacific Coast, established in 1891, and the third in the nation.

For more that fifty years a Chinese village thrived on **China Point** but went up in smoke quite mysteriously in 1903. Its settlers originally came to work in the Santa Lucia mines during Gold Rush days and drifted to the coast to resume a more familiar occupation, fishing. After the fire the Chinese established a community on Alvarado Street in Monterey.

Chinese junks followed the boat parade after the Feast of Lanterns, a tradition which began in 1880 at the close of each Chautauqua. This festival is held every year during the last week of July and is based on an Oriental legend about villagers searching with lighted boats and lanterns for the Mandarin's lovesick daughter, who was forbidden to marry her peasant sweetheart and ran off to drown herself. The Feast of Lanterns recounts the story with a week-long, city-wide celebration, including a lantern procession, a lighted boat parade, and the crowning of Queen Topaz.

Pacific Grove has a pleasing blend of old-fashioned and contemporary architecture with many beautiful homes typical of both eras. Several movies with New England settings have utilized Victorian homes here. The gazebo at La Porte Mansion (formerly Pinehurst Manor), 1030 Lighthouse Avenue, was built by Warner Brothers in 1958 during the filming of *A Summer Place*, starring Troy Donahue and Sandra Dee.

Redwood plaques designate nearly two hundred homes built in Pacific Grove before 1890. A two-day Victorian House Tour is held each March so visitors can view interiors of some of these restored turn-of-the-century homes. A sampling of these proud mansions will be noted here as you travel along. It's easy to find your way around. If you get lost in Pacific Grove, just head toward the water and you will be back on your itinerary.

Green Gables faces three directions on three levels

Pryor House, the three-story shake manor at 429 Ocean View Boulevard, was built in 1908 for twice-Mayor John P. Pryor. The promontory off Berwick Park, just ahead, was named after him. The foundation of the house and surrounding wall are of massive hand-hewn stone. Pryor House was featured in the television version of Steinbeck's *Winter of Our Discontent,* starring Donald Sutherland.

When **Green Gables Inn,** on the corner of Fifth Street, was erected in 1888 as a summer home by a Pasadena judge, it was called Ivy Terrace Hall. Vines cascaded from this Swiss Gothic down to the waterfront. It has been authentically restored as a guest house. Note that it faces three directions on three levels.

The gray castle-like home a few doors up from Ocean View Boulevard on Seventh Street is known as **Kinswood Tower.** It was built in 1889 by Everett Pomeroy, who created a small replica of his family's castle, Berry Pomeroy, in Devonshire, England. The distinctive crenelated square towers resemble battlements.

The **House of Seven Gables Inn** at 555 Ocean View Boulevard is another example of Victorian style and elegance, authentically restored and refurbished.

Roserox Country Inn, 557 Ocean View Boulevard, was built in 1906. It was once the home of feisty former Mayor Julia Platt, who gave it its name.

The large house at 110 Tenth Street was built by the Pacific Improvement Company in 1893 to be rented during the summer Chautauqua series. Originally it was closer to the water but was moved to higher ground in 1909.

Let the kids out to run at **Berwick Park,** the large grassy area on the shoreside between Hopkins Marine Station and Lover's Point, great for tossing frisbees or playing touch football or just loafing.

Lover's Point Park just ahead has picnic facilities, a volleyball court, children's pool, and access to the sheltered beach. This is one of few safe wading and swimming beaches on the

Monterey Peninsula. Be forewarned; the water's cold! In spite of the nippy average fifty-five degree temperature of the surface, hardy skindivers enjoy this spot, and surfers skim the huge waves when they break off the point. Rock fishing is good on the far side of the pier. Once there was a large bathhouse, a Japanese tea garden, skating rink, bowling alley, even a windmill, at Lover's Point. All are gone.

Many national publications have featured Pacific Grove's **Magic Carpet of Mesembryanthemum.** A glorious mass of pink and lavender ice plant, interspersed with clumps of geraniums, marguerites, red hot pokers, veronicas, tea, and yucca trees, blooms from late April through August along the cliffs between Hopkins Marine Station and Lighthouse Reservation. Winding paths and benches invite strollers. Hayes Perkins, a retiree, began planting the colorful ground cover across from his home in 1943 because it grows well in poor soil and requires very little maintenance. The city fathers took note of his successful experiment, and a crew was hired to complete the planting along the waterfront. Seeing the *Mesembryanthemum floribundum* in bloom at **Perkins Park** can make your whole visit to Pacific Grove worthwhile!

The three-mile shoreline is spectacular any time of the year, equally as beautiful as Seventeen-Mile Drive, and free to see. Pacific Grove is one of few California cities that owns its own shoreline. Because of continuing beach erosion and the disappearance of many small marine animals in recent years, collecting of all kinds is prohibited on these beaches. Park at the turn-out points. Don't feed the squirrels and chipmunks, or you may need a tetanus shot. Look for sea otters playing in the kelp beds and the huge white grandpa seal lounging on his private rock, and the interesting formation dubbed the **Kissing Rock.** You can scramble down to the water, but be extremely cautious. THE SURF IS UNSAFE; the undertow is quick and treacherous. If you feel like walking, there is a safe path through **Esplanade Park** between the street and beach from Lover's Point to Lighthouse Reservation with welcome benches along the way.

The oldest lighthouse in continuous operation on the West Coast, Point Piños

Eighteen hole **Pacific Grove Golf Links,** the only city-owned course on the Monterey Peninsula, is a fairly easy course and the least expensive of the public ones. Little **Crespi Pond** at its edge is a sanctuary for a variety of land and sea birds and is notable because it is a freshwater pond, yet very close to salt water. Also, look for the herd of Columbian black-tail deer roaming the golf greens.

If you have little ones along, you might turn left at Lighthouse Avenue, go a few blocks, and drive through **El Carmelo Cemetery.** This isn't as mournful as it sounds. The entire Peninsula abounds with wild life, and you may see families of deer nibbling at flowers in front of headstones.

It was the explorer Sebastian Vizcaíno who gave this headland the name "Point Piños" (Point of Pines). A sperm whale lamp first shone at **Point Piños Light Station** in 1855 and was replaced in 1880 by a kerosene lamp. In 1915 the lamp was electrified; now a thousand watt bulb, magnified by lenses and prisms, produces a fifty thousand candlepower beam visible for fifteen nautical miles under favorable conditions. The now-automated light is forty-three feet above ground and eighty-nine feet above water. A standby generator automatically takes over during any power interruption. This is the oldest lighthouse in continuous operation on the West Coast and was a landmark for galleons taking the north circle route down the California coast to Mexico. The tower was damaged extensively in the disastrous 1906 earthquake and had to be rebuilt; the building, plus the old French Fresnel lenses and prisms still in use, are the originals, The station houses a small museum of Coast Guard history and is one of few lighthouses along California's three hundred plus miles of coastline that is open to the public. You may visit any Saturday or Sunday from 1-4 p.m. Near the shore is the air diaphragm horn signal, also automated, which me-

Asilomar State Beach

thodically comforts Pagrovians during foggy nights. Being on the road next to it when the foghorn blasts will give you a jolt, to say the least.

Lighthouse Reservation is a preserve for rare plants and a refuge for migratory birds and marine and land animals. The sandy setting has a foundation of granite, geologically eighty million years old: some was quarried for building the Light Station. Among the rare beach flora are lovely blue Tidestrom's Lupine, one of the rarest, and butter-yellow Menzies Wallflowers.

Beyond Point Pinos, the site of many pre-radar shipwrecks, you will be on the ocean side of Pacific Grove. A herd of seals, an otter or two, and sometimes a sea lion inhabit the rocky cove of **Moss Beach.**

Adjoining the city is **Asilomar State Beach and Conference Grounds,** 105 acres of sand dunes and pine trees. Here thousands of conventioneers gather annually. The Conference Grounds were founded by the Y.W.C.A over seventy years ago, but now belong to the State of California and are run by Asilomar Operating Corporation, a non-profit organization. Asilomar (pronounced ah-seel-o-mar) means "refuge or retreat by the sea." Because famed architect Julia Morgan, who designed Hearst Castle, planned the original buildings and laid out the grounds, Asilomar has been declared a National Historic Landmark. One of the finest conference centers in the country in a beautiful setting of forest and sea, Asilomar is unique in the State Park system.

The California State Department of Parks and Recreation operates **William Penn Mott Center,** a training facility, the first of its kind, at Asilomar. This center provides formal classroom training for State rangers and park employees, with courses lasting one to five weeks. The curriculum is so complete that other states often send students here, and the National Parks Service contracts for training, also. East Woods houses a research library for scholars. The Center was named for the former head of all California parks, who is now Director of the National Park System.

"Doc" Ricketts gathered specimens from the "Great Tide-pool" mentioned in *Cannery Row* at Asilomar Beach. There are over 210 species of algae, more varieties than any other spot on the coast, because the northern and southern waters merge here. Please remember that California State law makes it illegal to collect any tidal invertebrates in State parks, recreation areas, and State beaches and reserves. No general collecting is allowed between the mean high tide mark and a point one thousand feet beyond the low tide mark offshore. Flowers, rocks, plants, animals, and other natural features are protected by law. Drift-wood may be collected from State beaches because it is not considered part of the natural environment.

You will be traveling east on Sunset Drive, State Highway 68. **First United Methodist Church,** a quarter of a mile from Asilomar at the intersection of Sunset Drive and Seventeen-Mile Drive, was built in 1963 on a five-acre wooded site where deer nibble, squirrels scamper, birds sing, and frogs croak. The original Methodist Episcopal Church , which doubled as a town hall in the Retreat days, was in the downtown area and torn down in the early sixties. While contemporary in appearance, the present church uses historic architectural forms and symbols. The mosaic-paneled front doors portray some of the major events of Christianity. The inspirational stained-glass "Resurrection Window" above the altar features parts of monarch butterfly wings. You are welcome to visit the sanctuary of Pacific Grove's founding church or attend Sunday services. If you are nearby just before noon any day, stop and listen to the person-played carillon as it fills the air with music.

Following Highway 68 (Holman Highway) will lead you back to Highway 1, but you won't want to miss the rest of Pacific Grove; so turn left at Forest Avenue. You will pass two large retirement residences on either side: **Canterbury Woods,** operated by Episcopal Homes Federation, and **Forest Hill Manor,** under the auspices of California-Nevada Methodist Homes, Inc. Continue down the hill to Lighthouse Avenue.

This is the middle of the downtown shopping area. There are no parking meters and, incidentally, no traffic lights downtown.

The green awning at 568 Lighthouse Avenue flags the entrance to **Pacific Grove Art Center.** Visitors are welcome to enjoy the galleries and studios where painting, sculpture, graphics, and other creative arts are displayed in a Victorian setting. Hours are 11 a.m.- 5 p.m., closed Sunday and Monday.

On the corner of the next block on the other side of the street is a branch of Eureka Federal Savings, which houses the **Bear Flag Museum.** Rare photographs, paintings, documents, and artifacts depicting Monterey County history are showcased. The displays can be seen during office hours, Monday through Friday, 8 a.m.- 5 p.m.

A short block up Seventeenth Street at the corner of Laurel, you'll find **Ketchum's Barn** with adjoining outhouse. Constructed in 1891 by H.C. Ketchum, it is now headquarters for the Pacific Grove Heritage Society. This small museum houses many historical materials, including photographs, oral histories, and memorabilia. Hours are: Saturday 1-4 p.m. year-round, and Wednesday-Friday noon-4 p.m. (May through September only). Admission is free.

Several of the city's finest old homes are along this main street. **Gosby House Inn,** 643 Lighthouse Avenue, was built in 1887 by a cobbler, J.E. Gosbey, who also ran a boardinghouse for Methodist ministers. (The "e" was accidentally dropped from his name when a new sign was painted a few years ago.) Later the Victorian was converted into a fourteen-room hotel and stayed that way for some seventy years; more recently it was renovated to become a bed-and-breakfast inn.

Next door at 649 Lighthouse Avenue is **Hart Mansion** (a restaurant). Dr. Andrew J. Hart, a dentist, had the house built in 1892. The first floor was his office, and the family used the second and third floors as their home. Notice Dr. Hart's leaded sign over the front door and the beautiful stained-glass and stencilled windows. Gosby House Inn and Hart Mansion are

A Pacific Grove dowager, Hart Mansion

examples of Queen Anne architecture with their gabled roofs, angular bays, turret towers, and porches set inside the main structure frames.

In 1880 the Methodist Bishop brought seed pods of euca-lyptus trees from Australia, and they were planted in a double row along "Lighthouse Road." Some of the largest blue gum eu-calyptus trees can still be seen in front of the Post Office at Lighthouse and Congress Avenues.

Several elegant old homes in the business section have been rescued for use as professional offices; 721 Lighthouse Avenue is one. The Nova Scotian cobbler who built Gosby House also built this attractive house in 1898. The turn-of-the-century interior provides a charming old-fashioned atmosphere for modern-day offices.

Holman House, 769 Lighthouse Avenue, was erected in 1889 for the owners of the area's only department store. The landmark mansion and its contents were willed to the Monterey

Peninsula Museum of Art to be used for historical and educational purposes. Following extensive renovation, it is now headquarters for the Museum on Wheels, an educational outreach program, and for the docents' Creative Response activities, bringing art education to schools, and also for workshops and meetings of related groups.

If you go back and walk toward the water on Forest Avenue, you will come to the **Pacific Grove Chamber of Commerce,** just a block below Lighthouse. The office is open from 9 a.m.-5 p.m. The staff will be happy to answer your questions and provide free brochures. An up-to-date street map of the entire Monterey Peninsula is inexpensive, and you will find good use for it later at Pebble Beach and in Carmel.

Along the way is one of the first houses built in Pacific Grove, 164 Forest Avenue. Many small cottages and some larger homes were built over original tent platforms. When this two-story, no-nonsense frame house was constructed around 1884, the canvas tent was left inside the walls as insulation. The boxy style and stick-work porch are typical of cottages built at the time.

The name of the double-turreted old hotel at 612 Central Avenue was a combination of the Spanish words *estrella* (star) and *Central*. **Centrella House** served as headquarters for Methodist ministers and their families when they came to participate in the retreats. It is one of the city's oldest hotels, built in 1888, and has been restored as a bed-and-breakfast inn.

Only 177 museums throughout the United States and Canada have been accredited by the American Association of Museums; the **Pacific Grove Museum of Natural History,** at the corner of Forest and Central Avenues, is one of thirteen in California to receive such accreditation. As long ago as 1935, the Association called it "the best of its size in the United States." Children will want to have their pictures taken astride "Sandy," the forty foot, eight thousand pound life size sculpture of a gray whale by Larry Foster, which lounges at the entrance.

The museum features marine and bird life, shells and Indian artifacts, and has a labeled native plant garden outdoors. A unique exhibit explains the fascinating phenomenon of the monarchs' migration. There are over four hundred mounted specimens of Monterey County birds in the collection. A relief map of Monterey Bay shows the great submarine canyon on its floor, eighty-four hundred feet down, a gash deeper than the Grand Canyon. This tremendous chasm is one of the reasons why Monterey Bay has always been a fishing port. Upwelling waters bring nutrients to feed surface organisms which in turn provide food for the bay's fish. Visiting hours at the museum are 10 a.m.-5 p.m. Tuesday through Sunday with free admission.

Pacific Grove Public Library, also on Central Avenue, was the first to be established in Monterey County in 1880. Their collection of over 1,250 volumes pertaining to the South Seas is the most comprehensive of its kind in the West, and contains many rare works, including those by explorers Hakluyt, Vancouver, and Cook, ancient maps and atlases, even handwritten logs from clipper ships and windjammers. Library hours are: Monday-Thursday, 10 a.m.-9 p.m.; Friday and Saturday, 10 a.m.-5 p.m.; and Sunday, 1-5 p.m.

In the late 1800s **Caledonia Park,** just off Central Avenue, was filled with tents occupied by people attending the Methodists' annual retreats. Tentsites are now places for playground equipment, welcome benches, picnic tables, and restrooms.

Another good sit-down spot is the top floor of Ford's Department Store on Lighthouse Avenue where you can enjoy a panoramic view of Monterey Bay. Formerly Holman's, once the largest store between San Francisco and Santa Barbara, this emporium has served the Peninsula since 1891 and was mentioned in *Cannery Row*. For a number of years John Steinbeck lived in a cottage in Pacific Grove, built by his father around 1900. Much of his research for *Cannery Row, Sweet Thursday,* and *Tortilla Flat* was done here.

There are five municipally owned tennis courts and a pro shop up the hill behind the **Community Center,** 515 Junipero Avenue. Children can exhaust themselves at the playground here before climbing back into the car. More tennis courts are located at the high school on Sunset Drive, available when school is not in session.

Washington Park (twenty acres) on Sinex Avenue at Alder Street, has complete picnic facilities including barbecue grills, plus a baseball field. There are lots of trees, many with butterflies in them during the season.

Now that you have a whole roll of film of Pacific Grove, "the change-of-pace place" on the Monterey Peninsula, reload your camera. It's time to see Pebble Beach and the world-renowned Seventeen-Mile Drive.

CHAPTER THREE

WORLD-FAMOUS SEVENTEEN-MILE DRIVE, PEBBLE BEACH

Pebble Beach, where stately mansions hide in verdant woodlands and emerald fairways meet sapphire sea, is not a vast private residential park by accident. This greenbelt and majestic beach front, totaling eighty-four hundred acres, were acquired in the early 1900s by Del Monte Properties Company (now Pebble Beach Company) under the presidency of the late Samuel F. B. Morse, great-nephew of the developer of the Morse Code. The company has strict building codes governing the preservation of the area's beauty and bounty of nature. Guidelines for the six thousand-plus residents and for visitors have been established for the protection of native flora and fauna. Rules prohibit disturbing plant or animal life of any kind.

Under Samuel Morse's leadership, buildings erected within Pebble Beach's boundaries were to be "Spanish-Colonial or Monterey style of architecture." Cypress Point Club, designed by George Washington Smith, is a perfect example of the Monterey style Morse had in mind. With the passage of years, rules about building have been relaxed. Now there are homes and mansions varying in style all the way from Colonial to Mediterranean to futuristic.

The original Seventeen-Mile Drive, planned sixty years ago, began and ended at the Old Del Monte Hotel in Monterey (Naval Postgraduate School) and encircled the entire Monterey Peninsula. It was more like thirty-five miles when President

Theodore Roosevelt made the trip on horseback in 1903. Now the Drive is routed only through the confines of Pebble Beach Company's land.

The exclusive atmosphere of the area is obvious right away. There are toll gates at each of the four entrances to this impressive community. Country Club Gate and Seventeen-Mile Drive Gate are in Pacific Grove; Carmel Hill Gate is midway up the hill from Monterey off Highway 1; and the one in Carmel is just plain Carmel Gate off North San Antonio Avenue. Residents have special license tags and come and go freely. Others must pay the $5 entrance fee (well worth it) to see the world-acclaimed **Seventeen-Mile Drive.** This gate fee is refundable if you plan to dine or stay at The Lodge at Pebble Beach (formerly Del Monte Lodge) or The Inn at Spanish Bay. If you have friends who live inside the gates, phone and ask them to call the security guard at the gate you intend to enter, and you will be admitted free of charge. There is a well-marked bicycle route along the Drive; bicyclists are required to get permits at the gate and are not allowed during weekends or on holidays. Traffic laws are strictly enforced on Pebble Beach property.

You will be provided with a map of Seventeen-Mile Drive showing points of interest along the yellow-and-orange painted line when you pay the gate fee, but do not stray too far from this designated route unless you have a complete map showing all roads, or you are sure to get lost and spend several hours trying to find your way out. The natives are friendly, though; so ask a pedestrian or knock on a door and the butler will gladly direct you.

From Seventeen-Mile Drive Gate in Pacific Grove, below the First United Methodist Church at Sunset Drive and Seventeen-Mile Drive, the road follows the low, white sand dunes and winds through exclusive residential sections, past showplace homes of some of America's most prominent citizens. You'll recognize their names on the gateposts. The coastline changes

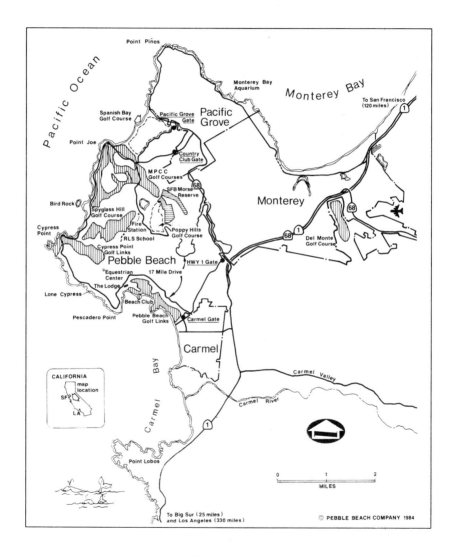

Seventeen-Mile Drive, Pebble Beach

from sandy dunes to jagged crags where ships have met their doom. Gnarled, wind-blown Monterey cypress trees, which grow indigenously nowhere else in the world, offer unusual subject matter for camera buffs. Huge offshore rocks are populated by resting birds and relaxed seals; deer graze unconcernedly on lawns and golf greens. In the spring mother seals teach their babies to swim in the sheltered coves. A sudden geyser of water ejected from the ocean, followed by a visible dark hump, denotes the presence of a passing whale during spring or winter. Shaded picnic areas, miles of winding bridle trails, coves of quiet beauty, and stretches of sandy shore enhance Pebble Beach. Many sites are described on the back of your map.

The Inn at Spanish Bay, stretching along 236 acres of beachfront, is a new addition to Pebble Beach Company's holdings. Bordering The Inn is an eighteen hole par seventy-two Scottish-style public golf course covering 195 acres and designed by golf experts Tom Watson, Sandy Tatum, and Robert Trent Jones, Jr. Eighty townhouses are also included in the complex.

Several shipwrecks have occurred at **Point Joe** because on stormy nights navigators mistook it for the entrance to Monterey Bay. Beyond is "the restless sea," where an unusual turbulence happens because of the configuration of the ocean floor.

The barren offshore outcroppings are called **Bird Rock** and **Seal Rock** and host lots of gulls and cormorants, seals, and sea lions. Granted, it's a smelly stop, but you'll enjoy a closer look at the animal and bird life through the stationary, mounted field glasses.

The thirty-eight acre campus of **Robert Louis Stevenson School** is off Forest Lake Road. This private college preparatory, independent secondary school was founded in 1952 for boys in grades nine through twelve, but now girls are also registered.

According to Fanny Osbourne Stevenson's memoirs, Robert Louis Stevenson drew on his vivid memories of walks along the Drive for descriptions in his immortal classic *Treasure*

Island. He described these twisted trees as "ghosts fleeing before the wind." Each of the holes at **Spyglass Hill Golf Course** is named after one of Stevenson's fictional characters, such as, "Long John Silver," "Blind Pew," and "Jim Hawkins."

The much-photographed **Lone Cypress** is the most famous of its species, Monterey cypress (*Cupressus macrocarpa*). Its survival against the elements and vandalism has been aided by guy wires. Undaunted in its struggle, this rarest of trees has managed to perpetuate itself by producing a young cypress growing out of its roots. Unsuccessful attempts have been made at transplanting Monterey cypress trees, but they will thrive only in this restricted habitat at the bleak headlands on either side of Carmel Bay. This is the only place in the world where you can see stands of these remnants of the Pleistocene Age. In protected **Crocker Grove,** the indigenous cypress, which have a lifespan of one hundred years, retain their normal straight and tall characteristics. Washed by sea spray and lashed by winds, they cling tenaciously to the rocky shoreline of Cypress Point and become misshapen and grotesque.

Pescadero means "a place where fishing is done." **Pescadero Point** forms the northern arm of Carmel Bay. On foggy nights the diaphanous figure of "the Lady in Lace" has been seen wandering near the bleached-bone-white **Ghost** and **Witch Trees.** It is assumed that this wraith is the restless spirit of Maria del Carmen Garcia Barreto Madariaga who once owned and twice sold Rancho El Pescadero which extended from Seal Rock to Carmel, now some of the most expensive property anywhere in the world.

Thirty-four miles of riding trails wander through Pebble Beach's glorious tree-and-sea setting. Twenty-seven acres of woods and grassy fields along Portola Road are the grounds of **Pebble Beach Equestrian Center.** In the early 1920s the stables here were used by Del Monte Hotel Guests. Through the years horsemanship has become a happy pastime for many Peninsulans. The Equestrian Center sponsors a full season of events:

18th hole at Pebble Beach Golf Links

shows, meets, races, and the "game of kings," polo. **Collins Polo Field** is across the way, where teams from all over the country gather for the National Rugby Championship every March.

Dominating the dramatically laid out golf courses along the natural shoreline is **The Lodge at Pebble Beach** with its fancy restaurants and exclusive shops. Elite groups such as **Cypress Point Club, Beach and Tennis Club,** and **Stillwater Yacht Club** rule the Pebble Beach social scene. **Monterey Peninsula Country Club** is on its own lovely knoll in Del Monte Forest.

The Lodge at Pebble Beach is one of the world's great resorts and has played host to a passing parade of celebrities. The John F. Kennedys vacationed here before he became president. Golfing presidents have always taken time out to swing their clubs at Pebble Beach. Surrealist painter Salvador Dali spent a series of summers at The Lodge. The antics of Dali, Oliver

Hardy, and W.C. Fields, who sauntered onto the golf course, drink in hand, cigar in mouth, and umbrella overhead, still provide table talk during dinner parties. Clark Gable was one of The Lodge's regular guests, getting in a little golf between pictures.

Golf can be enjoyed 365 days a year on championship courses: Pebble Beach, Cypress Point, Morterey Peninsula Country Club's shore and dunes courses, Spyglass Hill, Spanish Bay, Poppy Hills, and Peter Hay Par 3. Pebble Beach, Spyglass, Spanish Bay, and Peter Hay Par 3 are open to the public. Major tournaments, like the annual televised Pebble Beach National Pro-Am, are played on these challenging courses. Pebble Beach Golf Links were chosen as the site of the 1972 and 1982 U.S. Opens.

The Crocker Marble Palace

The late Jack Neville, a member of the winning U.S. Walker Cup team at St. Andrews, Scotland in the 1923 tournament, designed Pebble Beach Golf Links along with Douglas Grant. Neville, although not a golf architect, laid out the course over half a century ago, and it is still considered famous, or infamous, for its great climax, the eighteenth hole. Speaking of the eighteenth, Neville said: "The worst thing you can do is hook because it's ocean all down the left side."

George Washington Smith, designer of Cypress Point Clubhouse, also planned the **Crocker Marble Palace,** the car-stopper as you approach Pebble Beach through the Carmel Gate. It is the first waterfront mansion you see, recognizable by its many arches. Also called "Byzantine Castle," this ornate baroque mansion is one of the most notable along Seventeen-Mile Drive and was built and decorated between 1926 and 1931 for Mrs. Templeton Crocker of the railroad and banking family. Later she married Paul Fagan, an entrepreneur in California and Hawaii, and for a while the house was called "Crocker-Fagan Mansion." The interior is mostly of Italian marble with mosaic floors, marble baths, archways, and loggias. There are forty-five different arches in the garden, using thirty-two types of marble. Another extravagant feature is the beach heated by underground pipes. It is said that leftover marble was unceremoniously dumped into the water below when the house was completed.

Some of the stately homes along the Drive have hand-carved signs at their portals indicating how their owners' fortunes were made. "Wit's End" still identifies the home of the late cartoonist, Jimmy Hatlo. There is a spool of thread on the signpost at the entrance to the Coats' residence, of Coats and Clark fame.

Many Pebble Beach estates, now too costly for private ownership, have been sold or leased to large corporations and are maintained year-round as guest quarters for V.I.P.s or vacation retreats for executives.

As much as you have read or heard about this scenic wonderland, now that you have seen it, you will agree that Seventeen-Mile Drive rivals the Riviera and has managed to exceed your expectations.

CHAPTER FOUR

COZY-CARMEL-BY-THE-SEA

Indefinable Carmel-by-the-Sea is a captivating village that is really "by-the-sea." The city traces its heritage back to 1602 when Sebastian Vizcaíno, after claiming Monterey for Spain, camped for a month near Carmel River before sailing away to report his new discoveries to the King of Spain. Vizcaíno named the sea and the land after the Carmelite monks who accompanied him on this voyage. Carmel was first settled in 1771 when Padre Junipero Serra moved the Mission from Monterey to the more arable setting of Carmel. Most of the neophytes were Costanoan Indians.

The village proper, less that a square mile in size, didn't really burgeon until the early 1900s when it attracted a colony of artists, authors, and musicians. Their nonconformist way of life still prevails in Carmel. The 1906 earthquake left many of San Francisco's bohemians homeless. Poet George Sterling and novelist Mary Austin urged them to follow their lead to Carmel. Their small homes were nestled in the forests and edged the sandy beaches. Mary's tiny "winter wickiup" with a treehouse workroom in a close-by pine was near the Mission. A group of citified professors built vacation cottages; one was David Starr Jordan who later became the first President of Stanford University. One of the blocks of Camino Real is still referred to as "Professors' Row."

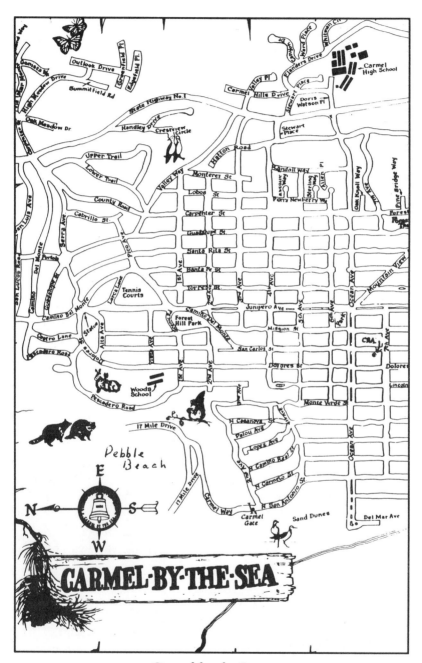

Carmel-by-the-Sea

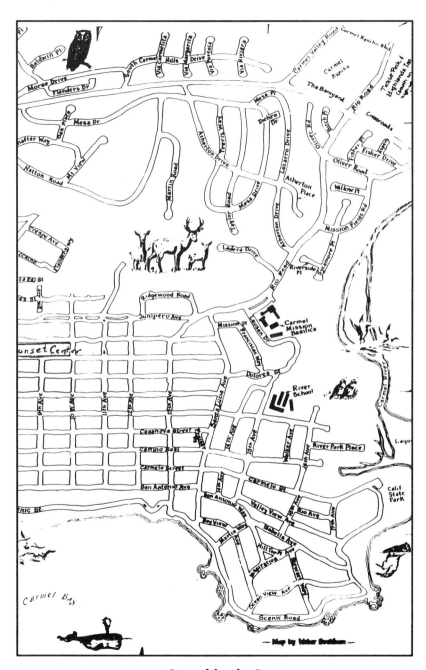

Carmel-by-the-Sea

Among the distinguished writers associated with Carmel's early days were Jack London, Sinclair Lewis, Jimmy Hopper, Upton Sinclair, William Rose Benét, and Robinson Jeffers. For awhile it was the home, too, of the talented and prolific Belgian mystery writer, Georges Simenon, who created the famous character "Maigret," a French criminologist. Also, there is a house on San Antonio Avenue still called "Lincoln Steffens House" even though it has changed hands many times. Steffens was a feared, muckraking journalist who developed an absolute phobia for noise in his later years and retired to Carmel before his death in 1936.

Well-known artists who appreciated the soul-searching solitude and stimulating beauty of Carmel were Jules Tavernier, Arthur Hill Gilbert, and Percy Gray. Stanton Delaplane, newspaper columnist and former Carmel resident, wrote: "Most of Carmel's storekeepers were artists. While packaging eggs, they gave little lectures on the effects you could get with gouache."

This diversified group set a pattern for preserving their surroundings that is still rigidly observed. One of the township's first acts was to draw up an ordinance to protect the trees. Rather than felling a tree when the winding streets were laid out, the planners simply split the road to curve on both sides of the cherished tree. This puzzles yet delights visitors whose hometowns may be concrete jungles. Showing utter disdain for progress, Carmel's latter-day pioneers decreed that there would be no streetlights nor sidewalks in residential districts. Nowhere would there be high-rise buildings or neon signs, and commercial ventures would not sully the wide white beaches. Even AAA signs and public telephone booths are custom-made to suit Carmel's rules. This means that while Carmel is notable for other facilities, it has no traffic lights, no parking meters, no courthouse, no jail, no cemetery, and no mortuary.

The log of laws passed by Carmel's governing boards over the years, often with humor and always with thoroughness, has kept casual charm under control. Take Ordinance 60 passed in 1925 under a section entitled "Obnoxious Industries Zone No.

IV." Obnoxious industries included were "stables, soap factories, match factories, chemical works, sawmills, and other industries of similar character."

A few years ago city fathers approved an ordinance prohibiting outdoor displays of "plastic plant materials or other simulated plant materials." It has to be the real thing — no imitations for Carmel!

Ex-Mayor Perry Newberry, a former San Francisco journalist, was one of the leading crusaders for preserving the city's unique independence. To keep progress from spoiling Carmel, he suggested installing toll gates at its entrances! He felt that home mail deliveries were unnecessary, and to this day many villagers go daily to the friendly-staffed Post Office at Fifth and Dolores to pick up their mail and exchange pleasantries with fellow citizens. Reading the bulletin board around the corner at the Post Office will give you an insight into the Carmel way of life.

Because of city officials like Newberry, there are no honky-tonk strips of motels, gas stations, nor hot dog stands. In 1929 a zoning law ruled that business development should be forever subordinate to the residential character of the community. Carmel-by-the-Sea, with a present population of five thousand, remains a charming collection of flower-bowered cottages and regal residences in the heart of a pine forest bordering Carmel Bay.

Carmel has always enjoyed a certain national popularity; however, the village received world-wide attention when actor Clint Eastwood announced his candidacy for the office of mayor in the 1986 election and over-whelmingly won. Eastwood has lived in Carmel off and on and has owned property here for some thirty years. He is also one of the partners in The Hog's Breath Inn, San Carlos and Fifth Avenue. The famous mayor's popularity increased when, shortly after taking office, he purchased Mission Ranch, a dining and entertainment spot, to keep the property from the hands of developers. When Eastwood came to Fort Ord as a soldier in 1951, he said he had spent enjoyable evenings at the Ranch, and when he returned years later, he was glad to find it still the same. "I love that feeling — it was as though time stood still," he said, expressing the sentiments of many Carmel old timers and newcomers as well.

From Highway 1 there are two entrances to Carmel: Carpenter Street and Ocean Avenue. Taking the Carpenter Street entry, at the first signal light if you are driving south, will take you through a residential area, a proper introduction to this one-of-a-kind village. When you reach the "Y" a short way down the hill, take Serra Avenue until you come to "the statue." Once it was suggested to the city council that this weathered oak sculpture of Padre Junipero Serra by Jo Mora be moved to a more

His Honor

Jo Mora's statue of Padre Serra

suitable location where it wouldn't be threatened by errant drivers. Residents protested loudly that Carmel-bound visitors would lose their way if they didn't have Padre Serra to guide them, so here he stays. Jo Mora was commissioned by Samuel F.B. Morse, who established Pebble Beach, to carve this statue in 1922. Mora, a native of Montevideo, Uruguay, studied art in New York and Boston and moved to the Monterey Peninsula in 1920 when he was assigned to design and execute the much-admired sarcophagus of Padre Serra at Carmel Mission. Mora died in 1947, and in that year was one of only eight persons whose names had been included in *Who's Who in America* since the book's inception.

"Turn left at the statue," Carmelites have been directing visitors for over half a century, and follow Junipero Avenue to the business district.

Typical Comstock architecture

Houses in the village proper have no numbers, so their distinctive architecture is a great help in finding a friend's home for the first time. Architectural emphasis has always been on individual expression. Even service stations are pleasing to the eye, some in Spanish style, others with modern Oriental overtones. One thing is certain: there is no such thing as typical Carmel architecture. There are redwood board-and-bat homes, adobe dwellings, sturdy log cabins, Spanish villas with high-beamed ceilings and flagstone floors, ultramodern mansions designed by world-famous architects, and then there are the Hansel-and-Gretel houses designed by Hugh Comstock. The latter have given Carmel its most lasting sobriquet: "A Storybook Hamlet." The Tuck Box, a tearoom at Dolores and Seventh Avenue, has this touch of Grimm and is an outstanding example of Comstock's dollhouse period.

Hugh Comstock built a large doll–like house for his wife, Mayotta, so she could display and sell her handmade "Otsy Totsy" rag dolls, Friends found the fairy–tale shop so "adorable" that Comstock was commissioned to build full-scale houses similar to it. These storybook-illustration homes are easily spotted along Carmel's winding, wooded streets. Comstock later perfected waterproof adobe bricks and built houses of these, with redwood shakes and hewn timbers adding character.

Other architects responded to natural settings, designing seashore homes with a Mediterranean influence. English cottages (one with an imported thatched roof, across from Carmel Mission), and New England salt boxes stand side by side.

A thatched-roof cottage across from the Mission

Plan to spend a whole day in Carmel: if you don't you will wish you had! Instead of having to run back to your car and move it every hour or two to avoid a ticket, park several blocks north or south of Ocean Avenue, the main business street, where there are no limited parking signs. Free public parking lots are located at the northwest corner of Dolores and Fifth, and at Sunset Center, two and one-half blocks south of Ocean Avenue on San Carlos. There is a pay-parking garage at Carmel Plaza, Ocean Avenue and Junipero.

Public restrooms are located on the third floor of Carmel Plaza, in Devendorf Plaza, at the corner of Junipero and Sixth, as well as in Harrison Memorial Library, Ocean and Lincoln Avenues, and in City Hall, Monte Verde and Ocean.

Carmel is for walking, browsing, and shopping, filled with hidden courts which could never be discovered while driving. You might do well to wear tennis shoes or low-heeled shoes as some sidewalks are not paved and have dips and protruding tree roots.

Carmel Business Association is the village's chamber of commerce. Their office is upstairs in Vandervort Court on the west side of San Carlos between Ocean Avenue and Seventh. Ask for a free copy of a Carmel map. A complete guide is available for $1 and includes information if you're planning a wedding in Carmel. The Association's office is open from 9:30 a.m. to 4 p.m., Monday through Friday.

Carmel's champagne-in-a-teacup atmosphere charms both young and old and provides a welcome escape from the hasty pace of big cities. There is something about the scintillating sunshine, contrasting tender mists, and downright fogs that makes even the retired put aside the idle life. Carmel-by-the-Sea is a community of everyday-and-Sunday painters, poets, potters, and putterers. In Carmel society you may find the attractive matron who checked your groceries in a gourmet market during the day sitting across from you at an elite dinner party in the evening.

Civilized, friendly Carmel-by-the-Sea is a city of serendipity. You have to do the exploring and discovering yourself. Window-shop along the main streets, of course, but meander back into arcades and courts, too. Be sure to look up or you will "underlook" some of the most interesting shops.

From a great hamburger to the finest French cuisine, there is a place to dine to suit every taste and every pocketbook. Public eating and drinking on streets or beaches is greatly discouraged, however. Unless you relish engrossing conversation or maybe a game of darts, chess, or checkers in a cozy bar, night life is nonexistent in Carmel. City law prohibits live entertainment, even juke boxes, in hotels, restaurants, and cocktail lounges.

There are few independently owned hotels left, and Carmel has one of them. Guests used to arrive at the **Pine Inn** on Ocean Avenue by stage. This is Carmel's oldest inn and has been a part of the village scene for three generations.

La Playa Hotel at Camino Real and Eighth, four blocks from the business district has been a part of Carmel's tradition since the early part of the century when it was a huge private estate. The many couples who have honeymooned here over the years often return to celebrate anniversaries.

Rest at **Devendorf Plaza,** the park off Ocean Avenue which was named for one of the town's first developers, J. Frank Devendorf. He and another entrepreneur, Frank H. Powers, acquired most of the acreage now known as Carmel in 1902. They leased and sold lots, preferably to people with artistic inclinations, for "a few dollars down and pay the balance when you can." Devendorf and Powers were interested in the arts and supported institutions like the Arts and Craft Club, formed in 1905, and **Forest Theater** at Mountain View Avenue and Santa Rita, one of the first open-air theatres in the country "whose pillars are primeval pine and whose roof is the sky." A concave hillside gives every seat a perfect view of the stage. Forest Theater was constructed in 1910 and has been presenting Shakespearean productions, plays, and concerts ever since.

Numerous fine art galleries show and sell the works of local artists and artisans and those of other artists from all over the world. You can watch weavers, potters, and sculptors at work in their own studios. There are close to one hundred galleries and studios, each as absorbing as the next. Hotels, motels, and galleries all have free walking guides to simplify finding these artistic spots.

As the number of artists increased in the 1920s, it became evident that they needed a showcase. In 1927 a group of painters formed the **Carmel Art Association,** and then came the Depression. Meetings and exhibitions were held in members' galleries. Finally in 1934, the Association purchased an old studio at Dolores and Sixth Avenue and renovated it into handsome gallery rooms. It is open from 10 a.m.-5 p.m. daily.

A private art school, **Carmel Art Institute,** 28500 Hatton Road, was founded in 1938 by Armin Hansen and Kit Whitman. Guest lecturers and teachers, such as Fernand Leger, Alexander Archipenko, and Frederic Taubes, have appeared here. The school was purchased later by Pat and John Cunningham, both artists. Mr. Cunningham was involved in one of Carmel's most enigmatic happenings. In the early 1940s he invited a San Francisco sculptor, the late Beniamino Bufano, to attend the opening of the Bach Festival. When Bufano's large stainless steel statue of Bach, especially executed for the occasion, was due to be unveiled, it was discovered that the eight hundred pound bust had been spirited away. To this day it has never been found.

Cherry Foundation at Guadalupe and Fourth is a combination art gallery, schoolroom, and performing arts center. The gallery is open 2-4:30 p.m. Wednesday through Sunday. Carl Cherry invented the Cherry rivet gun, which makes blind riveting without explosives possible, and proved invaluable during World War II ship-and-plane building. The Cherry rivet made the Foundation, a lifetime dream of Cherry and his artist wife, Jeanne D'Orge, a reality.

The village's annual attractions range from kite-flying and sand castle building to the glorious two-week long Annual Bach Festival held in July at **Sunset Center** at San Carlos and Ninth. This Festival, now in its fifth decade, is the largest and most popular live classical music event within easy reach of Pacific Coast residents, and enjoys the patronage of many out-of-staters. Sunset Center's theater, with its excellent acoustics, good parking, and proximity to lodging and dining facilities, is the perfect setting for this auspicious event. Some Festival concerts are held at Carmel Mission Basilica with its magnificent organ, nearly two thousand pipes strong, a blending of musical technology, of old and new.

Sunset Center is often referred to as the "Jewel of Carmel" because of its outstanding cultural and artistic activities. This cultural complex has an assembly hall which seats 750 and various other meeting rooms which accommodate 40 to 250 people. The studios offer short-term instruction in various art forms for visitors. The galleries and studios are open to the public.

Carmel Beach

The **Church of the Wayfarer** on the corner of Lincoln and Seventh Avenue has a Biblical garden, a pleasant place to pause and gather knowledge at the same time. Plants, shrubs, and trees are labeled with their common and generic names and with chapter-and-verse references to the Bible.

Sometime during the day, you are bound to say: "But where's the beach?" It's at the foot of Ocean Avenue, and on a clear day you can see the ocean from the top of the hill. Walk a few blocks straight down Ocean Avenue and you'll be there. **Carmel Bay** is between Cypress Point and Pinnacle Point. The beach is wide, white, and sandy. Sunbathing and picnicking are favored pastimes; SWIMMING ISN'T SAFE.

From early morning until late at night on the Fourth of July, Carmel's beach is crowded with picnickers. Sometimes a whole neighborhood or an entire club membership comes together. A day that grows foggy has never kept Carmel's citizenry from celebrating their independence. The beach front glows with campfires as night falls.

On Twelfth Night (twelve days after Christmas), Carmelites bring their dismantled Christmas trees to the foot of Thirteenth Avenue. A gigantic fire blazes on the beach while hundreds of onlookers participate in the traditional ceremony marking the close of the Christmas season and the beginning of Epiphany. The light of the fire heralds the start of a new year; the tides swallow remnants of the old.

The Great Sand Castle Contest is an event begun in 1962 just for family fun, free of written rules. The exact date is never announced until a few days before, but it's usually held in early fall. Categorical prizes and sour grapes awards are given by judges who are local architects. Entries range from the profile of an ex-President to a full-sized Volkswagen. Sometimes there are no castles at all for the tide to wash away.

You won't want to miss **Scenic Road** along the tree-bordered bay of Carmel Mission Basilica. Drive toward the beach on Ocean Avenue and turn left on Scenic Road. Go

Hawk Tower at Tor House

slowly along this narrow, twisting, street and enjoy the views on both sides— enviable homes and enticing beaches.

Poet Robinson Jeffers' **Tor House** and adjoining **Hawk Tower,** constructed entirely of granite found along the shore, are the most striking of the many architectural styles in Carmel. The stone house was patterned after an English Tudor barn Jeffers had seen and admired. The forty foot, three-story tower, built as a musical retreat for his organist wife, Una, is an adaptation of an old Irish tower. Two portholes salvaged from a local shipwreck were installed in the walls. Jeffers, a semi-recluse, came to Carmel in 1914 to devote full time to writing. Much of his poetry bears a direct relationship to the natural landscapes of this coastline. People come from all over the world to see this fabled stone house, including many from Czechoslovakia where Jeffers developed an almost cultlike following.

Tor House Foundation, a non-profit organization, along with the National Trust for Historic Preservation, purchased the house, tower, and property in 1979. Docent-led tours are conducted Fridays and Saturdays between 10 a.m. and 3 p.m. Advance reservations are necessary; call 624-1813.

Harrison Memorial Library at Ocean and Lincoln has an extensive, valuable collection of selected works by Robinson Jeffers.

Local tour guides are no different from their breed elsewhere and like to season their lectures about important sites with a little spice about scandals. They point out the love nest on Scenic Road called **Benedict Cottage,** where famed evangelist Aimee Semple McPherson spent ten days with her then-current amour, Kenneth G. Ormiston, a former radio operator at her Temple. Believing her concocted tale that she had been kidnapped from her ornate Angelus Temple in Los Angeles, police from all over California searched for Aimee until her tryst in Carmel came to light. She was later indicted by the Grand Jury on a false kidnapping charge.

Walker House on Carmel Point was designed by Frank Lloyd Wright. Jutting out on a rocky arm and surrounded by water on two sides, it appears to be an intrinsic part of the natural surroundings, like all of Wright's masterpieces.

Scenic Road rounds the point and becomes Carmelo Street. Turn right on Fifteenth Avenue which will lead to the **Basilica of Mission San Carlos Borromeo del Rio Carmelo.** Built in 1771, this Mission was Padre Junipero Serra's headquarters until his death in 1784 and his favorite of the nine he personally founded. He is buried at the foot of the altar. The first adobe church was replaced by a larger stone edifice in 1797 under the direction of Padre Fermin de Lasuen. In 1834 the Mexican Government, then ruling California, ordered the secularization of the Missions. The Franciscan Fathers were sent back to Spain, and Carmel Mission, without their guidance, was abandoned in 1836. The Indians , who tended the corrals, vast grazing lands for sheep and cattle and farming acreage, were left homeless and helpless and became scattered throughout the territory. Typical of these was "Old Gabriel," whose grave is in the small cemetery in the Mission courtyard. At the time of his death, he was considered "the oldest man in the civilized world." More than three thousand Indians are buried in the cemetery beside the church.

The first steps towards restoration of Carmel Mission took place under Father Ramon Mestres in 1924. The late Sir Harry Downie, renowned authority on California Mission architecture, along with Father Michael D. O'Connell, took over and completed the task. Since 1933 the Mission has been a parish church.

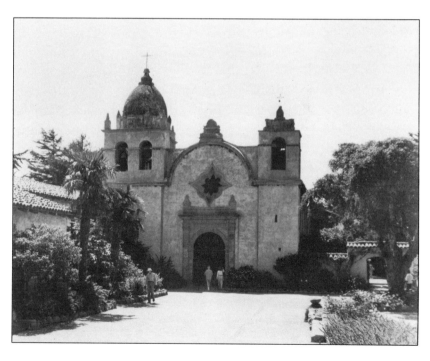

Basilica of Mission San Carlos Borromeo del Rio Carmelo

The stateliness of the Mission's early days interwoven with the Peninsula's past is obvious the moment you push open the bare wooden door leading to a courtyard reminiscent of Spanish-Colonial times. The impressive stone church has a splendid exterior tower adorned with Moorish-style star window and dome. The massive redwood gates invite all to come to worship or study or admire the church and well-kept gardens and court-yard.

There are two museums on the grounds supported by voluntary contributions. They are open from 9:30 a.m.-5 p.m. weekdays, and 10:30 a.m.-5 p.m. Sundays. The array of practical and religious treasures reveals the hardy, industrious and austere lifestyle of Padre Serra and the Franciscan monks who were his contemporaries. The kitchen and tiny modest room where Serra slept have been reproduced.

Ignoring the electronic marvels of modern science, the art of campanology has been revived at Carmel Mission. Seven workable bells, some dating back to the early 1800s, are rung by pulling ropes, the same way it was done over two hundred years ago.

In 1960 Pope John XXIII elevated Mission San Carlos Borromeo del Rio Carmelo to the highly dignified rank of Basilica, one of only eleven churches so designated in the United States and one of only two Basilicas in the western states.

Several parks add to Carmel's charm. **Mission Trail Park,** a thirty-five acre sanctuary covering the area between Carmel Mission on Rio Road at Lasuen Drive and Mountain View Avenue, has a walking trail extending from the south end of Forest Road near Forest Theater all the way to Rio Road near the Mission. Part of this trail is the same path Padre Serra trod with Indian converts from the Mission to Monterey to obtain necessary supplies. The three main trails in the park are: Junipero Serra (.08 miles), Flanders (.05 miles), and Doolittle Nature Trail (.04 miles). Mesa Trail is an offshoot of Serra Trail and leads upward to a breathtaking vista with the Mission in the distance. Flanders Trail leads to Lester Rowntree Arboretum and Flanders Mansion. The Arboretum is a showcase of California's native plants, nurtured by the local chapter of the California Native Plant Society. It is best to remain on marked paths as they are surrounded by persistent poison oak.

Forest Hill Park is on the outskirts of town in the woods below the road leading along Camino Del Monte. It offers an imaginative children's playground, horseshoe pit, shuffleboard court, and besides asphalt walking and jogging paths, a nine-station parcourse.

CHAPTER FIVE

PASTORAL CARMEL VALLEY

In the late 1800s Robert Louis Stevenson described Carmel Valley in *The Old Pacific Capital* as "a true Californian valley, bare, dotted with chaparral, overlooked by quaint unfinished hills. The Carmel runs by many pleasant farms, a clear and shallow river, loved by wading kine." Novelist Mary Austin chose this region as a setting for *Ysidro*, her story of Mission days in quiet Carmel Valley, and John Steinbeck's paisanos hunted frogs in the river's marshes.

Many Indian artifacts have been found on Carmel Valley ranches. Long ago tribes moved up and down the valley, to and from the coast according to the seasons. Early settlers acquired their acreage through Spanish and Mexican land grants. As early as the 1830s, the pasture lands were divided into enormous privately held grants: Rancho Cañada de la Segunda, Rancho Potrero de San Carlos, Rancho San Francisquito, Rancho Los Laureles, and Rancho Tularcitos.

The sixty-four thousand acres of this unincorporated drowsy valley, stretching fourteen miles east of Carmel, are surrounded by the steep beginnings of the rugged Santa Lucia Mountains to the south and high ridge of the Peninsula to the north. The fourteen thousand residents live in homes varying from the unpretentious to the pretentious; some sprawl graciously along the Carmel River banks while others hang by their chimneys on the cliffsides.

Rancho San Carlos, Carmel Valley

Carmel Valley's climate is warmer than elsewhere on the Peninsula, so the landscape is punctuated with resorts, restaurants, theaters, equestrian, tennis and golf facilities — some public, others posh and private. The hotels and motels are more than just places to stay overnight; all offer a variety of interesting activities. There are large orchards and truck gardens, dude and cattle ranches. Roadside stands have fresh fruits and vegetables grown in the valley, and along Carmel Valley Road are a Christmas tree farm, begonia gardens, a succulent farm, and a chicken ranch where you can buy newly-laid eggs.

Carmel River flows thirty miles northwest through the coastal ranges to south of Carmel. Steelhead season opens in mid–November and runs through February. Whether or not fishing is good depends on rainfall and the amount of water released by the Los Padres and San Clemente Dams upstream. If you are over sixteen, you will need a license for freshwater fishing.

The Barnyard at the mouth of Carmel Valley

Deer and mountain lion hunts and special wild boar hunting expeditions are conducted in the Santa Lucia Mountains. In 1919 Russian wild boars were brought to this country from the Ukrainian Mountains to a hunting preserve on the border of North Carolina and Tennessee. Thirteen boars were shipped to Monterey County in 1924. They mated with runaway domesticated swine, and hundreds now roam the far regions of the Santa Lucias. Boar hunting is not for beginners; the average boar weighs 250 pounds, a dangerous and fast prey.

The entrance to the valley is a few miles south of Carmel to the east of Highway 1. Neighboring shopping centers at the mouth of the valley, Carmel Center, Carmel Rancho Center, The Barnyard, and The Crossroads are connected by a road at the rear. Picnic fixings can be purchased at the supermarkets or delicatessens here.

Rancho Cañada Golf Club (public), a mile east, has two side-by-side courses winding back and forth over five bridges across Carmel River, clubhouse facilities, pro shop, bar, and dining room.

You will go by the entrances to two adult communities, **Hacienda Carmel** and **Del Mesa Carmel,** and a retirement community, **Carmel Valley Manor,** operated by Northern California Congregational Retirement Homes, Inc., before you reach mid–valley.

The impressive French castle at 8940 Carmel Valley Road is **Chateau Julien,** a wine estate set on seven picturesque acres extending to the Carmel River. This is a small boutique winery with a twenty-five thousand case capacity, producing about 70 percent white wines and 30 percent red. Tours are by appointment only.

On the north side of the road, opposite Via Mallorca, is **El Encino del Descanso** (The Oak of Repose). Christian Indians stopped to rest under this time-bent oak while transporting their dead to Carmel Mission for burial.

The award-winning architecture of **Quail Lodge,** adjoining **Carmel Valley Golf and Country Club** (private), is worth seeing. The notices posted on the sides of the buildings at neighboring Valley Hills Shopping Center will give you an insight into the rural feeling of the area.

Turning right at Schulte Road will lead first to **Riverside Park** and then to **Saddle Mountain Recreation Park** beyond, both with recreational vehicle facilities, campsites, and picnic facilities. This locale was first an Indian campground because of the adjacent river, and later a Mexican land grant to Loretta Onesmina de Peralta in 1837. Saddle Mountain, a mile in from Carmel Valley Road, has a three and one-half mile hiking trail leading to an elevation of one thousand feet for a superb view of Moss Landing, the Santa Cruz Mountains, and Los Padres National Forest.

An unobtrusive sign on Schulte Road marks the entrance to **Aquatica Water Gardens,** where the beautiful Japanese fish, koi, are cultivated. These exotic fish are shipped all over the country, along with water lilies, lotuses, and water hyacinths. Early June is a good time to see the flowers in bloom. This three-acre piscicultural garden is open to the public.

Berwick Barn on Berwick Drive is a Carmel Valley landmark and has captured the imagination of local artists and photographers for many years. Changing its face and color with the seasons and even with the time of day, the barn never appears the same in any two paintings. Englishman Edward Berwick raised this picturesque building in 1869 as the first improvement on his 120 acre ranch, where he cultivated Winter Nelis pears which became world-famous and were shipped to many European markets. In the early spring, fragrant white blossoms can be appreciated here and there on the few remaining pear trees which were once a part of huge orchards. **Berwick Manor and Orchard** has been nominated for inclusion in the National Register of Historic Places. Much of the original Berwick homestead, which was purchased for $500 in gold, has been sold off; twenty-nine acres remain. The first home, part of which dates back to the 1840s, has hand-hewn beams tied with rawhide. The Berwicks entertained Robert Louis Stevenson several times. but he was always banished to the barn to sleep because the hostess was suspicious of his eczema-scarred hands and consumptive cough.

Carmel Valley Riding and Polo Center on Robinson Canyon Road offers professionally guided trail rides for the entire family. Guides will escort riders high into the mountains and meadows along the river banks. Small–group rides are geared to individual levels of proficiency.

The **Korean Buddhist Temple, Sambosa (Three Treasures),** just off Robinson Canyon Road, is situated on seven and one-half secluded acres facing the gently flowing river with serene mountains as a backdrop, a setting similar to that of its sister temple in Seoul, Korea. The unusual shade of lavender on the Temple's façade is characteristic of the Korean sect of Buddhism. The natural wood structure is Oriental in theme and

Cabin where Robert Louis Stevenson was nursed back to health

spirit, gracefully blending East and West. Serious students come here for one hundred day retreats involving intensive meditation. The public is invited to attend regular Sunday services at 11 a.m.

Robinson Canyon Road continues south through redwood groves and a cool, wooded canyon. About ten miles down the road, on the site of a former Angora goat ranch in the Santa Lucia Mountains, are the weathered relics of some wooden buildings. Robert Louis Stevenson lived in one of these tumbledown cabins for a short time during the fall of 1879. Suffering from "galloping consumption," which eventually caused his death, the author left Monterey to escape the penetrating fog and save on lodging expenses. After being thrown from his horse, Stevenson anguished under a sheltering tree for two nights before Anson Smith, a bear hunter, and Jonathan Wright, the goat rancher, found him. The two mountain men nursed Stevenson back to health. While recuperating, the famed author was moved to write this requiem: "Beneath the wide and starry sky, dig a grave and let me lie...."

A rustic sign eight and one-half miles out Carmel Valley Road, just before Los Laureles Grade intersection, marks the entrance to **Garland Ranch Regional Park** (twenty-four hundred acres), Carmel Valley's first park and the initial acquisition of the Monterey Peninsula Regional Park District. The gates are open from 8:30 a.m. until sunset. No motorized vehicles are allowed in the park, so stop your car in the designated area, then cross the footbridge. You'll probably want to take a picture of the 'TOAD CROSSING" sign on the footpath that alerts walkers to the swarms of baby toads during springtime. Trail maps and a bird identification pamphlet are available at the visitors' center, the frame building just across the river. Drinking water and restrooms are here. Miles of clearly marked nature trails offer hikers a choice of easy, short walks or an arduous climb to eight hundred foot high **Inspiration Point** for a panoramic view of the mountains and valley. Equestrian trails lead through oak and buckeye studded hills and broad mesas to mountain tops. There are picnic areas but no formal lawns, play equipment, nor barbecue pits. The beauty of this park is its total emphasis on nature at its best — wildflowers and wildlife in their natural habitat, hidden glades, expansive meadows, a waterfall, and lots of sunshine and fresh air. In all, this scenic parkland is a place to picnic, hike, ride, fish for steelhead, or just see and enjoy.

Los Laureles Grade goes north and connects Carmel Valley Road with State Highway 68, the Monterey-Salinas Highway, at a point about midway between Monterey and Salinas. The road is about six miles over the mountain tops with an all-encompassing view and has been designated a Scenic Highway, indicated by the California poppy symbols on road signs.

Continuing east on Carmel Valley Road, you will come to **Boronda Adobe.** Don José Manuel and Maria Juana Boronda built their home on the west side of Boronda Road, near its intersection with Carmel Valley Road, and in 1840 they became the first in-residence ranchers on huge Rancho Los Laureles. The once-crumbling adobe was altered and added to through the years and has been lovingly restored for use as a private residence. The old part is of interest architecturally. It is sixty-four feet long and nineteen feet wide, and the thick walls have been well-preserved.

Boronda Adobe

When her husband was crippled in a horseback-bullfighting accident, Doña Boronda turned to cheese-making to support their fifteen children. Using an old family recipe, she produced "Queso del Pais" (cheese of the country) and began marketing it. Some went to the Santa Lucia goldmines and some was used for trading in Monterey. Her venture was so successful that other dairy ranchers in the valley began making cheese, too, in order to use up excess milk. **The White Oak** Properties complex on Carmel Valley Road, between Paso Hondo and Esquiline Road in the heart of the village, housed the Boronda's dairy business. The white clapboard building with the odd cupola was a cooling house for milk and cheese. David Jacks, a canny Scotsman and leading Monterey businessman, discovered Maria's cheese. He owned several dairies that he leased on a share arrangement, so he started these farmers in the cheese-making business. Jacks' Monterey Cheese soon became known as "Monterey Jack Cheese." However, old-timers attribute the name to the heavy house jacks used to fasten the tops of the kegs in which curds were mashed in order to squeeze out the whey. Northern California is still the only place where Monterey Jack Cheese is manufactured.

Hidden Valley Music Seminars, an Institute of the Arts at Ford Road, was organized to bring young artists, students, and teachers together in the most productive environment possible. Five-week seminars are held during the summer to train young people for the professional world of music, including the opera. The dormitory behind the theater will accommodate eighty students. Musicals are presented at Hidden Valley and at Sunset Center in Carmel. The Children's Theater Division brings live professional productions into the classrooms throughout the Monterey Peninsula.

The **Madonna of the Village,** between Hidden Valley and the Post Office complex, spreads joy, peace, and love. The village is the business and social center of the valley. There are many craft and gift shops and art galleries to explore and several excellent restaurants in or near the village.

Robles Del Rio Airport, about a quarter of a mile north-east on El Cammito Road, is normally a fog-free, eighteen hundred foot airstrip suitable for single and light twin-engine planes.

On a hot summer's day, a dip in the Old Swimming Hole is a good way to cool off. Take Equiline Road, off Carmel Valley Road. The cliffs at **Porter's Cove,** north of Equiline Bridge, form a natural diving board for the swimming hole.

Beyond the village, Carmel Valley Road becomes Tularcitos Road. Turning south on Cachaugua (pronounced ka-shaw-wa) Road for about ten miles will take you to **Prince's Camp,** a privately-owned camp and mobile home park. In the 1920s this was an informal hunting and fishing campground with a small store and saloon.

Just beyond the turn-off to Prince's Camp is the entrance to **COMSAT (Communications Satellite) Earth Station,** situated on a 161 acre site. A thirty-four ton parabolic dish antenna, ninety-seven feet in diameter and standing taller than a ten–story building, is focused on a communications satellite 22,300 miles away. This is part of a network involving more than 130 countries and territories, so that important news events can be televised simultaneously around the world. Visitors may take guided tours between 1 and 3 p.m. Wednesdays. It would be wise to call ahead to let them know you are planning to come (659–2293). If the staff is short-handed, sometimes tours have to be cancelled. A brief movie concerning the operation of the Station is shown; then a technician explains the complicated electronic equipment, how the signal is received and transmitted to the satellite. The Earth Station is not classified; you may take pictures. Leave your pets in the car and keep track of your children. No picnicking is permitted on the property.

About five miles farther is **Los Padres Reservation.** Park your car near the Ranger Station and walk to the reservoir, owned by California-American Water Company, about half a mile on a dirt road. There is a U.S. Forest Service Park here. Trout fishing is good in season; only self-propelled boats are allowed on the lake. This park is crowded in summertime and on sunny weekends. Hiking is a back-to-nature experience, and this is one of the starting points to the profusion of trails throughout Los Padres National Forest. You must sign in at the Ranger Station, which is open daily from 8 a.m. to 5 p.m., if you intend to hike into the wilderness.

Cachagua Road joins Tassajara Road. **Jamesburg,** a small unincorporated settlement at the junction, was named after its founder, John James from North Carolina, in 1867. A monument on the site of the first Post Office honors the James family. The first settlers filed three kinds of claims: homestead, preemption, and timber, each 160 acres. This meant that individual family members could pool their 480 acre claims to make a fair-sized cattle ranch. Early cabins were built on sled runners so they could easily be moved from claim to claim. The settlers lived off the land for the most part. Winters were hard and when ready cash was needed, they trapped live grizzly bears and hauled them off to Monterey in oxcarts to be sold for bull-and-bear fights. They also gathered ladybugs by the handful in the caves at Chews Ridge and sold them to Salinas Valley farmers for use in their fields— the forerunner of modern pesticides. At the turn of the century when Tassajara Hot Springs, to the south, was a popular health spa, stagecoaches carrying vacationers left Salinas at 6 a.m. and arrived at Tassajara at 6:30 p.m., a distance of fifty-three miles, stopping at James Ranch along the way.

Hastings Natural History Reservation, on the north side of the Jamesburg-Arroyo Seco Road, encompasses two thousand unspoiled acres along Finch Creek. Once a working cattle ranch, the Reservation is now owned by the University of California and is managed by Berkeley's Museum of Vertebrate Zoology. Botanists and zoologists from around the world come to Hastings to study plant and animal life in a real environment away from laboratory conditions. Students and researchers stay from a few weeks to a few years. Since 1937 the forest and grazing lands have been left untouched to allow them to return to their natural state. You will understand why the Reservation is not open to the public, and picnicking, hunting, and domesticated animals are forbidden on the property. Visitors are usually ecology, college, or nature groups who come for tours and lectures.

From Jamesburg the road winds another six miles to **Chews Ridge,** the destination of many outdoor enthusiasts who come in the summertime to enjoy camping and hiking, and in the wintertime to try out their seldom-used sleds on the snow-covered slopes. From the ridge there is an eagle's-eye view of Los Padres National Forest, north to Salinas and west to Big Sur country and the Pacific Ocean. The caves near Chews Ridge were often used as shelter by the extinct Esselen Indians, a small tribe of only a few hundred. Writings on cave walls indicate that they were later inhabited by Costanoans who hunted wild game in the area.

The Santa Lucia Mountains provide some of the finest spots on earth for stargazing. The first independent astronomical observatory established since World War I, **Monterey Institute for Research in Astronomy,** is 5,060 feet atop Chews Ridge on a site leased from the U.S. Forest Service. The thirty-six inches reflecting telescope weighs six tons and was designed to withstand winds of more that 120 m.p.h. The sixty-foot wind turbine supplies some of the electrical power used by the observatory. This observation and research facility houses a computer control room, exhibit room, mechanical room, and dormitory. If you brought along your own telescope, this is a tremendous spot to use it because there are no artificial lights to compete with the heavens. Tours are offered Sunday afternoons at 1:30 and 3:30 when road and weather conditions permit. Reservations are needed: call 375-3220.

China Camp, south of Chews Ridge, has a Ranger Station and full facilities for overnight camping. Beyond here the road becomes more difficult.

Tassajara Hot Springs, at the end of the road approximately fifty-two miles from the mouth of Carmel Valley, deep in an isolated valley between the lofty Santa Lucia peaks, were known to the Indians and later to the Spaniards for their chalybeate qualities. The name "Tassajara" comes from the Spanish word "tasajera," meaning "a place where meat is cut in strips and hung in the sun to dry."—in other words, jerky.

From 1904 on, Tassajara became a fashionable retreat with a large brownstone hotel, which burned in 1949, and rustic buildings and bathhouses along Arroyo Seco Creek. For a distance of two hundred yards, seventeen hot mineral springs issue from the mountainside at a temperature of 140-150 F. The water contains sulphur, sodium, magnesia, iron, and phosphate.

The road into this forty-eight acre property was built in the 1880s by Chinese laborers. While the narrow road is much improved, it is still an hour-and-a-half drive from Carmel Valley village. It is winding, scenic, dusty, and somewhat precipitous, definitely a low-gear journey, through tree-thatched, untamed mountains.

In 1967 the Zen Center of San Francisco purchased Tassajara Hot Springs Resort, and it is now headquarters for Zen study and training in North America. New buildings have been added, and the mineral baths have been developed in the Japanese tradition. In the summertime visitors are welcome to come during daylight hours; families are most welcome. For a reasonable fee you can picnic and enjoy the baths. Overnight reservations must be made well in advance. The dining room is open to overnight guests only; emphasis is on simple vegetarian food. Fresh bread is their best-known culinary treat; there is a Tassajara Bread Bakery in San Francisco. Tassajara is closed to the public during winter months when the Center is used only for student training. Reservations during the rest of the year can be made at the Tassajara office in Jamesburg. The stage, a four-wheel drive vehicle, makes the trip once a day to the Hot Springs; the cost is $6 per person, one-way.

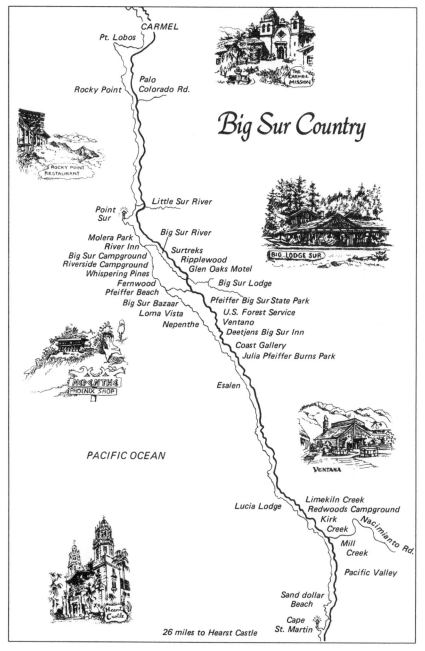

Big Sur Country

CARMEL
Pt. Lobos

Palo
Rocky Point   Colorado Rd.

THE CARMEL MISSION

Big Sur Country

ROCKY POINT RESTAURANT

Little Sur River

Point
Sur

Big Sur River

BIG LODGE SUR

Molera Park
River Inn   Surtreks
Big Sur Campground   Ripplewood
Riverside Campground   Glen Oaks Motel
Whispering Pines
Fernwood   Big Sur Lodge
Pfeiffer Beach
Big Sur Bazaar   Pfeiffer Big Sur State Park
Loma Vista   U.S. Forest Service
Nepenthe   Ventano
                  Deetjens Big Sur Inn

Coast Gallery
Julia Pfeiffer Burns Park

NEPENTHE
PHOENIX SHOP

Esalen

VENTANA

PACIFIC OCEAN

Limekiln Creek
Lucia Lodge   Redwoods Campground
               Kirk   Nacimiento Rd.
               Creek

Mill
Creek

Pacific Valley

Sand dollar
Beach

Hearst Castle   Cape
                 St. Martin

26 miles to Hearst Castle

Big Sur Country

CHAPTER SIX

BREATHTAKING BIG SUR COUNTRY

Big Sur is the name given to the ruggedly beautiful seacoast country stretching south from Carmel River to the southern Monterey County line. This now famous coast route is one of the world's most spectacular highways and an inspiration to poets, painters, and photographers. Seventy-two scenic miles connect the Monterey Peninsula with Southern California. Prior to the opening of Highway 1, it took half a day over a narrow, unsafe road through dense thicket and virgin timber to travel from Monterey to Big Sur. Before that there was only a horse trail for hauling supplies to the few inhabitants along the coast.

Highway 1 was built at a cost of $10 million, took sixteen years to build, and was opened in 1937. During its construction, men lost their lives and equipment plunged into the sea. The road was plotted to take advantage of the breathtaking views as it hugs the natural rocky-coved shoreline, twists along steep cliffs, spans canyons formed by rushing rivers, and ambles along foam-fringed ocean beaches. At some places the road ascends almost one thousand feet above sea level, then sweeps grandly around a point and descends to within fifty feet of a comely cove. The dramatic contrast between the restless, sometimes vehement sea and the serene beauty of primitive forests and magnificent mountains is unforgettable. Big Sur is an oasis in a day when wilderness is fast disappearing.

More species of birds are found in this coastal area than anywhere else in California. Many animals, from mice to mountain lions, thrive in its forests. The phantom white orchid grows high in mysterious canyons, while rare ferns and wildflowers lace the inland streams.

The first residents of Big Sur country were the Costanoans or "coast people," who hunted sea lions but lived mainly on a diet of fish and shellfish, supplemented with nuts, berries, and roots, seasoned with seaweed.

In Spanish "Sur" means south. Big Sur country took its name from Rancho El Sur, where early settler John B.R. Cooper and his family lived when they were not in Monterey. Cooper took the name "Juan Bautista Cooper" when he adopted Mexican citizenship. A shrewd trader, he accumulated much wealth and land, including Rancho El Sur.

The best time to drive Highway 1 is between noon and 6 p.m. when inspiring views are not shrouded in coastal fog. Be alert at the wheel; this road changes with the turns, the hours, the days, and the seasons. Make sure you have film in your camera, take your time, and marvel at the drama of each unfolding scene of this unduplicated seacoast called Big Sur. It's full of big surprises!

It's fun for children to play a game called "Count the Bridges" as you drive south on Highway 1. There are thirty-eight bridges of varying sizes between Carmel River and San Simeon Creek. The longest is Bixby Creek Bridge (714'), then Big Creek Bridge (589'), followed by Willow Creek Bridge (562'). Watch closely or you'll miss some of the shorter ones.

For over half a century, globe artichokes have been cultivated along both sides of Highway 1 on the flat plain near the mouth of Carmel River. The State purchased the western 155 acres next to the road which eventually will become a natural park. The view of the ocean from the highway will be preserved, and there will be no sophisticated developments, such as playgrounds or overnight campgrounds. Open space will be cherished and the environment protected, another milestone toward saving our precious land.

Bay School, the little red schoolhouse in an enviable acre-and-a-half setting of trees, sand dunes, and beach south of the artichoke fields, was built in 1879 to educate the children of whalers living at Point Lobos. The only other school at the time was in Carmel Valley, so many of the students arrived on horseback. The school had an uninterrupted flow of children through its doors for nearly a century. In 1952 it became a parent cooperative nursery school under the auspices of the Carmel Unified School District. When it was declared unsafe according to earthquake requirements, the termite-ridden little historical building had to be demolished when costs for restoration to meet those standards proved prohibitive. Concerned citizens rallied, and an exact replica was constructed on the same site in 1976.

The highway drops to sea level at **Monastery Beach,** a part of **Carmel River State Beach** (106 acres), which is crowded during good weather with swimmers, surfers, skindivers, sunbathers, and surf-fisherman. It must be noted that THE SURF IS UNSAFE here. The lagoon at the mouth of the river is better for small children. When the river is running, it is possible to paddle your canoe or kayak into the lagoon's marshes for bird-watching.

On the hillside is the **Monastery of Our Lady and St. Teresa.** From their rooms the nuns can gaze out across the mind-calming sea or contemplate the tree-covered hills behind their imposing home. They lead a strict, cloistered life, stressing poverty, seclusion, silence, and work, with prayer taking priority. Their lifestyle is little different from that of St. Teresa de Avila who renewed the then four hundred year old Order of Discalced (barefoot) Carmelites in 1562. A nunnery was established in a frame building on Carmel Point in 1925; the Monastery was opened here six years later. The sisters raise vegetables in their gardens, and their food supply is supplemented by many donations of fruit, eggs, cheese, and fish; they do not eat meat. Four beehives produce honey. For income the nuns stitch vestments, do sacristy laundry, and make gift items which are sold at the

Monastery of Our Lady and St. Teresa

Monastery and the Hermitage Shop in Carmel. The chapel is open to the public from 8 a.m.-5 p.m. every day. The sisters who greet you have not taken the optional vow of silence. People of all faiths are invited to attend Masses or Sunday benediction or just visit and renew their spiritual strength.

The nuns you may see enjoying the beach across the way are Sisters of Notre Dame, a teaching order. The smaller building near the Monastery is **Villa Angelica,** their summer home.

San Jose Creek is several hundreds yards south of the Monastery. Gaspar de Portolá and his men passed through this area in 1769, still trying to identify Carmel River and Monterey Bay on the basis of Vizcaíno's descriptions. Padre Juan Crespi offered mass in a nearby meadow where, on a previous expedition, Portolá had erected a cross and buried a letter beneath it lamenting his failure to find Monterey Bay.

Just south of the semicircular cove at San Jose Creek Bridge, where Japanese fishermen once harvested abalone, is the entrance to **Point Lobos State Reserve.** Artist Francis McComas described Point Lobos as "the greatest meeting of land and water in the world." It is said that Robert Louis Stevenson used Point Lobos as a model for Spyglass Hill in *Treasure Island,* the classic adventure tale he wrote for his stepson, Lloyd Osbourne, whom he loved very much. Words are inadequate; Point Lobos must be experienced.

To get the most from your visit to Point Lobos State Reserve, wear low-heeled shoes and comfortable clothing, take along a coat or sweater and remember your camera. Plan to spend several hours enjoying concentrated natural beauty. The park is open from 9 a.m.-5 p.m. daily, and until 6:30 p.m. in summertime. A map will be provided at the gate when you pay the $2 per car entrance fee. Hikers and bicyclists are admitted without charge unless they are planning a picnic. Very few roads mar this primitive area; most of it can be seen only on foot over unobtrusive trails. You can drive through the entire Reserve to trailheads and to the picnic area. There is no overnight camping. Swimming is permitted at China Cove, and boats can be launched at Whaler's Cove. Remain on the marked trails and enjoy all of Point Lobos for its unequalled beauty.

State Rangers conduct guided tours twice daily in the summer and on a lesser schedule off-season. Visitors are taken to six areas: Cypress Grove, Pine Wood, Bird Island, North Shore Trail, Whaler's Cove, or the sea lion area. In the summertime when weather and tides permit, there are early morning guided tidepool walks.

Point Lobos derives its name from its colonies of California and Steller's sea lions. You can hear their hoarse barking emanating from Punta de los Lobos Marinos (Point of the Seawolves). The California sea lion is the most intelligent of all of its kind and the one usually used in trained seal acts. The Steller is larger and less controllable.

Before white men came, Indians had overnight campsites at the Point while they fished and gathered abalone and mussels along the shoreline. Point Lobos has had a string of owners since. The first recorded owner of the area was Don Marcelino Escobar who received the property from the King of Spain. Story has it that during the Mexican regime, this natural wonderland changed hands in a card game and became the unofficial property of a group of Presidio soldiers. At various times it has been the site of a smugglers' cove, whaling station, abalone-drying yard and cannery, and a cattle ranch.

In the 1860s Portuguese whalers operated a station at Carmelo Cove (now Whaler's Cove). This was a foul-smelling business with huge hunks of whale meat on the dock, cauldrons of boiling blubber emitting dense black smoke, shouting men, and screaming gulls. The oil was shipped out to be used in lamps and machinery. Chinese fishermen built a cabin here before 1880, evidenced by remnants of their life found beneath the pine flooring. The restored cottage will become a rest center where visitors can learn about the human history of Point Lobos from such artifacts as old maps, dominoes, poker chips, cigarette papers, and parts of opium pipes. In the 1890s Japanese fishermen had an abalone cannery at Whaler's Cove.

Once Point Lobos had an unsuccessful coal mine. Gold and mineral mining ventures also failed. Rocks from a quarry here were used to build the United States Mint at San Francisco and Monterey's old jail behind Colton Hall. After that nature took over and covered with greenery the scars of mining experiments. Much later, following the attack of Pearl Harbor in 1941, the Army's Signal Corps was stationed here for nine months.

Land speculators had been eyeing Point Lobos with avarice for many years. In 1933, with the help of the Save-the-Redwoods League, the wind-swept point passed into the trusteeship of the State of California from the heirs of A. M. Allan, a man who appreciated the natural qualities of this well-preserved, almost primeval area. It is truly the crown jewel of the California State Park system. In 1968 the National Park Service designated this 1,250 acre Reserve a Registered National Landmark.

There are over three hundred species of plants and 250 species of vertebrates and invertebrate animals and birds in this outdoor museum. The Monterey Cypress, widespread in the Pleistocene era, is making its last stand in the Monterey Peninsula region. Only a half-mile strip is left in the world. There are two small areas where this famous tree still grows naturally, one at Pebble Beach and the other at Point Lobos. In the spring acres of wildflowers brighten the landscape. Sea otters are always frolicking offshore. Bird Island is a sanctuary for thousands of land and sea birds. Point Lobos is also the northernmost breeding ground of the California brown pelican. The conglomerate pebbles here, ranging in size from your thumbnail to several inches, are the only record known of rocks from the Eocene Period.

Weston Beach on the southern side was named after the late Edward Weston, who was nationally known for his beautiful photography of Point Lobos.

Point Lobos has the first undersea Ecological Reserve in the nation, 750 acres of submerged land. With permission, underwater studies are carried on by individuals, universities, and private research groups. Skindivers must obtain permits (for looking and picture-taking only) at the park entrance.

Point Lobos has been a favorite on-the-spot site of moviemakers for many years. In the 1920s and 1930s, scenes from *Foolish Wives*, *Evangeline*, and *Paddy, the Next Best Thing* were filmed here. The most recent was *Jonathan Livingston Seagull*. Stricter regulations are now in force to avoid endangering the land and life of Point Lobos.

It will be difficult to leave Point Lobos behind, but there is much more of beautiful Big Sur country to see. Spindrift Road, down the way, winds toward the ocean past a long-established residential area, Carmel Highlands, where costly homes cling

View from Highlands Inn

to rocky ledges and hang over the crashing surf. One of the area's most distinguished residents was the late Ansel Adams, famed nature photographer, who produced major exhibits throughout the country and authored more than thirty books.

Yankee Point has a superb view of the craggy coastline and is an especially good spot for whale-watching. In November you can watch California gray whales migrating to their breeding and calving areas in Lower California and see them return in the spring to their feeding grounds in the Bering Sea, an eleven thousand mile journey. These huge mammals are thirty to fifty feet long and weigh about a ton a foot.

Joseph Victorine sighted this point from a whaling vessel in the early 1860s and made up his mind to settle here. He returned to the East Coast, packed up his family, and moved out West. The Victorines settled on the site of the present Bay School but later built a home on this promontory where they established one of the first dairies in the area in 1899. Victorine sold out to a land development company in 1928, but it failed during the Depression. Another Yankee, Charles G. Sawyer, purchased the property in 1948, and Victorine Creek was renamed "Yankee Point." Sawyer subdivided, and elegant homes began cropping up on the precipitous cliffs.

Little Malpaso Creek doesn't seem too forbidding now, but early accounts tell of difficulties pioneers had crossing it. In fact, an angry settler named it "Malpaso" (bad crossing). Carmelo Land and Coal Company operated a mine in the canyon here until the early 1900s. The coal was hauled to Point Lobos to be shipped out.

From **Soberanes Point** south to Point Sur is a California Sea Otter Game Refuge. Sea otters were hunted for their valuable furs until they were nearly extinct. Now protected, their population has increased. You can see them cavorting about in the tangled kelp along the shore.

The path at Granite Canyon Bridge goes down to the sea where there is a small waterfall with natural arches and grottoes. The one-time Navy missile-tracking station in **Granite Canyon** is now a marine-tracking center called the **California State Fish and Game Mariculture Laboratory.** The research done here, studying mass cultivation techniques for seafood items, such as red abalone, Dungeness crabs, and Pismo clams, benefits both commercial and sport fishermen. The public is invited to visit the Laboratory during a one-day annual open house held in May.

The main attractions at fairly new **Garrapata** (wood tick) **Beach State Park** are quiet natural beauty and unobstructed vistas of the ocean with wildflower walks along the creek in the canyon in springtime and winter whale-watching. The Park, open from sunrise to sunset, has no amenities for picnicking, and parking is provided only at a few roadside wide spots. On weekends a Ranger leads walking tours along a three-mile trail, starting at the tin barn just inside the entrance.

Palo Colorado means "tall redwood" in Spanish. A paved road leads into this narrow canyon lined with redwoods and healthy ferns with cabins along the creek. It goes to **Bottchers Gap**, the beginning of many hiking trails into Ventana Wilder-

ness, and beyond to **Pico Blanco Boy Scout Camp.** At the helicopter landing, there is a striking view of Little Sur Valley,
Double Cones, and Pico Blanco in the Santa Lucia range.

Ventana Wilderness is in the heartlands of the Santa
Lucias, part of Los Padres National Forest. This area is accessible
only by trails. Hikers and campers need Wilderness Permits from
the U.S. Forest Service before starting out. The sanctuary is a
240 acre area ten miles south of Big Sur that can be reached
only from Coast Ridge Road. It is only for wildlife research and
is not open to the public.

Notley's Landing, across from the entrance to Palo
Colorado Canyon, was an early-day lumber boomtown and busy
seaport. Split redwood posts and pickets were loaded on boats
by ship-to-shore cables. Tanbark was also exported, as well as
lime from a kiln in the canyon. Old Notley's Landing was the
prototype for the setting of *Zandy's Bride,* starring Liv Ullmann
and Gene Hackman, but filming was done farther south at

Big Sur Coast

Molera Ranch. The story was based on a novel entitled *The Stranger* by the late Lilian Bos Ross, who lived on Partington Ridge with her husband, Harrydick Ross, sculptor and wood-carver.

Here you have a choice: Follow Highway 1 south over the bridge or take the Old Coast Road. Turning left on a narrow, winding, hard-parked road (generally impassable during wet weather) will take you on a loop through the hills behind ranchlands for a look at inland Big Sur countryside before returning to the oceanside route at Andrew Molera State Park. Local ranchers were tired of bringing in supplies by muleback or by boat to the landing below, so in 1880 each rancher agreed to build a section of the road across from his own property.

Bixby Creek Bridge is the most-photographed bridge along Highway 1 and the longest concrete arch span in the world, 714' long and 285' above Bixby Creek in the steep-walled canyon below. Originally it was called Mill Creek Bridge, then Rainbow Bridge, and eventually Bixby Creek Bridge. The creek was named after Charlie Bixby, a cousin of President James Knox Polk, who built a sawmill here and had a thriving lumber business until timber sources ran out. Bridge construction used up sixty-six cubic yards of concrete and 600,000 pounds of reinforcing steel. There are safe observation alcoves on this engineering feat which offer a fantastic view of the Pacific. This is another fine vantage point for whale-watching. The sea-lanes are fifteen miles out; with binoculars you may be able to see a freighter or two.

The ruins at **Castle Rock** at the northern edge of this canyon were the site of old Bixby Landing where Monterey Lime Company, at the turn of the century, transported lime from the ridge by aerial cables to the creek mouth. Depletion of the rich limestone deposit and heavy rains brought the operation to an end after four years. Robinson Jeffers used Bixby Landing as a setting for his narrative poem, *Thurso's Landing*.

Bixby Creek Bridge

In September 1966, Mrs. Lyndon B. Johnson dedicated Highway 1 as California's first Scenic Highway. A plaque was placed at the south end of Bixby Creek Bridge and promptly disappeared, was retrieved, and disappeared again. It was inscribed with Robinson Jeffers' words:

I, gazing at the boundaries of granite and spray,
    The established sea marks, felt behind me,
Mountain and plain, the immense breadth of the continent,
    Before me the mass and doubled stretch of water.

Hurricane Point is the windiest spot on the whole highway, so hang onto your hat! Be extremely careful, especially if you are driving a light car or a top-heavy camper or towing a trailer.

Pico Blanco (elev. 3,710') governs the skyline along the highway past **Little Sur River.** This river was called "Rio Chiquita del Sur" (Little River of the South). There is a lovely lagoon where it joins the sea, but it is all private property.

Looming ahead is **Point Sur Light Station,** built on a gigantic volcanic rock. Before the lighthouse started warning ships in 1889, many smashed against the treacherous rocks along the coast. During its construction, a steep half-mile road had to be cut into the massive formation for pack mules to climb. With pulleys and ropes, native stone, quarried near Little Sur River, was hoisted. Several small houses and a large stone house, living quarters for the lighthouse keeper and teacher, were also built. The small schoolhouse was 395 steps below the lighthouse. The causeway linking the Station with the mainland used to flood and turn the mighty rock into an island; a sandbar was built to curb the tides.

The elaborate glass prisms, through which the first kerosene lamp was amplified, were made in France and shipped around the Horn. This delicately balanced old lamp had to be retired in 1971 because maintenance was costly and time-consuming, and it has found a home at Allen Knight Maritime Museum at Custom House Plaza in Monterey.

Point Sur Light Station now has a powerful million-candlepower light, fifty feet above ground and 270 feet above sea level, visible for twenty-five miles. The foghorn blasts every sixty seconds when the coast is obscured. The Station is also equipped with a radio beacon synchronized with six others along the coast.

The Navy's dirigible *Macon* broke up and crashed off Point Sur in 1935. Quick action on the part of the lighthouse keeper resulted in the rescue of most of the crew.

The Light Station was operated by the U.S. Lighthouse Service until the end of World War II when the U.S. Coast Guard took over. The operation is entirely automated now. A mini-computer monitor is hooked up with the Coast Guard

Station at Monterey, and an electronic technician services the equipment at Point Sur. Tours of the lighthouse are available on a limited basis; for information call 667-2315.

Note that paved shoulders on both sides of the highway provide bicycle paths from Point Sur to Ventana.

The 2,154 acres of **Andrew Molera State Park,** between Highway 1 and the ocean, extend on both sides of Big Sur River to a point about two miles inland. This property was acquired by the State in 1965, a gift from Miss Frances Molera in memory of her brother. The Molera family's pioneer cabin dates back to 1834 and has been restored. Most of this bucolic acreage will always be maintained in its natural condition to preserve the scenic beauty. Hiking trails skirt the river or lead to the sea. Surfing and surf-fishing at the mouth of the river and freshwater fishing upstream are allowed. Leave your car on the highway shoulder; there are no roads inside the Park. Sunrise to sunset picnicking is allowed, but no open campfires. Walk-in overnight camping is permitted in a designated campground.

The Old Coast Road goes north out of Andrew Molera State Park over the mountain tops, coming out at the north end of Bixby Creek Bridge.

Ahead is **Big Sur Village.** The residents are a mixture of descendants of early settlers, business people catering to the tourist trade, Park and Forest Service employees, ranchers and farmers, artists, authors, and artisans. This rural community has no mayor and no town hall. Civic matters are settled at meetings held at the Grange Hall, which is also their gathering place for social events, movies, and square dances. The village was slow to acquire civilized amenities enjoyed for many years by Monterey Peninsulans. Electricity didn't reach some homes until 1945. News of the outbreak of World War II was brought by a modern-day Paul Revere on horseback.

Many kinds of accommodations and restaurants are available in the village, and most are open all year.

Catholic Masses are held every Sunday at **St. Francis of the Redwoods.** This unusual church has a movable glass wall, making it possible to sit indoors or out where amplifiers are hidden in the towering trees. Sunday services are also held year-round at **Santa Lucia Chapel** (Episcopal) in a six acre redwood grove.

John Pfeiffer was the first permanent white settler at Big Sur. His pioneer cabin is in **Pfeiffer Big Sur State Park.** He and his family had planned to find some good farmland farther south, but the winter of 1874 was so severe they were forced to remain in Sycamore Canyon on the west side of the highway. By spring they were settled in and decided to stay.

Pfeiffer Big Sur State Park (2,944 acres) has eighty miles of hiking trails through a sylvan setting watered by **Big Sur River.** This river is shown on early Spanish maps as "Rio Grande del Sur" (Big River of the South). Pfeiffer Park is also the hub for five hundred miles of trails through Los Padres National Forest, which encompasses ninety-eight thousand acres of wilderness. This forest is one of the few places where the Santa Lucia fir (bristlecone fir) grows naturally and is also the southernmost end of the natural range of coast redwoods.

Carmel, Arroyo Seco, Little and Big Sur Rivers run through Ventana Wilderness. There is a 645-mile patchwork of fishing streams with native trout and some with rainbow trout stocked by the State Department of Parks and Recreation.

Two sanctuaries have been established for the California condor, an extremely rare, endangered species; one is in Ventana Wilderness. The condor is the largest North American land bird, with wing spans up to nine-and-one-half feet, and it nests only every other year. The female lays a single egg, not in a nest but in soft earth in sandstone cliffs or bluffs.

Deer, wild boar, and an occasional black bear inhabit the forest, as well as numerous smaller animals. Grizzly bears were plentiful in Monterey Country at one time. Now the State Department of Fish and Game estimates there are between twelve and fifteen bears in the County, most in Los Padres National Forest.

Pfeiffer Big Sur State Park is a popular place for outdoor enjoyment, a favorite of campers, and always crowded in summer months and on good-weather weekends throughout the year. There is a day-use fee and campsite charges. Hundreds of campers are turned away, so reserve early. Reservations can be made by contacting any California State Park office. There are developed campsites, trailer facilities, group campsites, picnic areas, swimming and fishing in the river, and riding and hiking trails. Guided nature walks and outdoor community programs on summer evenings are among the many nature-geared activities at the Park.

Below Pfeiffer cabin is the rock-rimmed gravesite of the last Indian family to live at Big Sur. **Mt. Manuel** was named after Immanuel (Manuel) Innocenti, who was a vaquero for Juan Bautista Cooper, owner of Rancho El Sur. On a clear day, Mt. Manuel is the goal of many hikers. The trail climbs four-and-one-half miles to an elevation of thirty-one hundred feet for a splendid view of the coastline on one side and the vast wilderness on the other. Another trail leads to **Pfeiffer Falls** through a cathedral-like grove of stately coast redwoods.

Another path leads down to white, sandy **Pfeiffer Beach** and lagoon and its sea-carved caves. Take your coat; it's usually very gusty here. Busy sandpipers scurry back and forth eluding the tide. *The Sandpiper,* starring Elizabeth Taylor and Richard Burton, was filmed on this beach. Access to Pfeiffer Beach from the highway is about two miles south of the Park. A right turn-off will take you along a two-mile drive through a canyon and a tunnel of cypress trees to the beach, open from 9 a.m.-6 p.m. daily.

Big Sur Lodge is a State concession with hotel-type accommodations and housekeeping cottages, dining room, coffee shop, gift shop, and general store.

Fire permits, camping information, and forest regulations are available at **Big Sur Guard Station,** a quarter mile south of the State Park entrance. If you intend to hike into Ventana Wilderness, you must sign in here.

Big Sur's first Post Office and first school were at **Post Hill,** another bustling way station on the road from Monterey. William Brainard Post arrived from Connecticut in 1840 and was responsible for founding the small community in 1877. The renovated Post homestead, one thousand feet above sea level, is a reminder of those early days.

Nepenthe is defined as "a potion used in ancient times to drown pain and sorrow." The steep path from the parking lot is worth the climb to view the seascape from modern-day Nepenthe, 808 feet above sea level. This was originally a log house built by the Trails Club many years ago. Orson Welles once purchased it as a castle for his movie queen, Rita Hayworth, but she preferred the Aga Khan and never lived here.

A quarter of a mile south of Nepenthe in **Graves Canyon** is the **Henry Miller Memorial Library,** full of books, photographs, and other mementos of Miller's life and times, as well as those of other writers who lived here and wrote about the Big Sur coast. The famed, controversial author lived in Big Sur from 1944 to 1962. Emil White, a writer and painter of primitives, gave his rustic redwood home to the Big Sur Land Trust in 1981 to honor his close friend. The library collection also includes volumes concerning the history and geology of the area, Indians, marine biology, and native plants and animals.

The sandy beach at **Castro Canyon** is populated by sea lions. They bask in the sun and splash in the surf. Don't try going down the cliff; the rescue patrol will probably have to haul you up!

Stop on the oceanside across from **Grimes Canyon.** You may hear the barking of a huge herd of seals seven hundred feet below. This is another sheer drop-off, so be careful.

Many years ago Harry Lafler, a former editor, made his home in the hollowed-out trunk of a redwood tree at **Lafler Canyon** and later in a one-room house built from marble quarried from his land. Now two round redwood tanks house an art gallery on this site.

Drive carefully over **Torre Canyon Bridge;** the curves are sharp. The cluster of mailboxes on the road belong to families living atop **Partington Ridge.** John Partington was aboard the S.S. *Venture* when it wrecked off Point Sur in 1879, strewing its cargo of wagons and linens along the coast. He decided to settle on this ridge and make a living by hauling tanbark and timber.

Jaime de Angulo, cowboy, anthropologist, medical doctor, professor, and author, lived on Partington Ridge in the 1920s and 1930s. He shared the beauty of his land in death as he did in life. **De Angulo Trail** was bequeathed to the U.S. Forest Service and leads to the top of Partington Ridge for a great view of the raw coastline. It is three miles to Coast Ridge Road, four miles to Cold Springs Camp, and nine miles to the south fork of Big Sur River. This is a mountainous trail and should be attempted by experienced hikers only.

Peaceful **Julia Pfeiffer Burns State Park** (1,725 acres) was named in honor of a Big Sur pioneer who came here with her parents from Marin County in 1869. Julia married John Burns, another long-time resident; they leased Saddle Rock Ranch and adjoining pastureland and lived at **McWay Canyon.** Their barn above the picnic area is an example of early redwood construction. Some of the ridges in this ruggedly beautiful park rise to three thousand feet with dramatic overlooks of the magnificent coastline. Redwoods dominate the park, interspersed with tanoaks, madrones, and laurels. Shade-loving ferns and wildflowers edge inland trails. Often seen are deer, raccoons, gray squirrels, possums, and gray foxes. Though here, rarely seen are mountain lions, coyotes, bobcats, and wild boar. A steep path leads to a small beach at the mouth of the creek, another old tanbark dock. A pedestrian underpass goes to a spot overlooking the waterfall at Saddle Rock where **McWay Creek** plummets fifty feet into a cove where there are rafts of sea otters. This is the only known waterfall on the West Coast to empty into the ocean. A two-and-one-half square mile offshore underwater reserve protects marine life in the area. Experienced diving groups may get permission at Big Sur Guard Station to dive along this part of the coast. There are two picnic areas along the waterfall trail near the parking lot and restrooms. Julia Pfeiffer Burns State Park is open from 8 a.m. to sunset.

In pioneer days this Park was Saddle Rock Ranch, owned in more recent years by Lathrop Brown. The **Tin House** high above the fog line was supposed to have been built for Franklin D. Roosevelt as a quiet retreat for writing his memoirs after his term as President. Brown, who was Roosevelt's life-long friend, constructed the unusual house in the early 1940s with materials from three abandoned gas stations. Unfortunately, the president did not live long enough to write his story in the Tin House.

California State law made prisoners available for highway work on a paid basis. Some of the convicts who helped build Highway 1 lived in shacks near Anderson Creek and Kirk Creek to the south. From here work proceeded in both directions. Later **Anderson Landing** became an art colony with authors and artists in residence.

Located at Old Slate's Hot Springs overlooking the Pacific is **Esalen Institute,** known nation-wide for its programs to expand human potential. The sign at the front gate reads "By Reservation Only;" however, the natural hot springs are open to the public, for a fee, Monday through Friday.

John Little State Reserve (twenty-one acres) is open for daytime use but has no facilities as yet. Fog hangs over this spot in the summertime; when clear, the view of the coastline is tremendous. Livermore cabin in this park is a board-and-batten structure made of split redwood that was brought by sled from Soberanes Canyon around 1921.

At least seven hundred years ago the Esselens probably watched Cabrillo and Vizcáino making their way up the coast to explore California. Diggings have shown that an Indian village with a population of around one hundred flourished near **Big Creek Bridge** (589'). Nature Conservancy has been responsible for preserving four thousand acre Big Creek Ranch, which spreads for four miles along the coast and reaches up six thousand feet to the highlands of the Santa Lucia Mountains. One of the southernmost stands of redwood trees in the world is here, plus a pristine watershed, natural springs, several streams, and a remarkable diversity of plant life and an equally diverse wildlife population. The ranch has been transferred to the University of California for use as an outdoor laboratory for teaching and research in ecological and biological studies.

The highway curls south to **Gamboa Point, Lopez Point,** and the little town of **Lucia** where Wilbur and Ada Harlan homesteaded in 1885. These self-reliant settlers raised ten children, and members of the third generation of the Harlan family still live at Lucia.

A mosaic sign by the roadway marks the entrance to the only American branch of the Benedictine Order, an Order which has fewer than 150 members throughout the world. This is the former Lucia Ranch, thirteen hundred feet above sea level. **New Camaldoli** (pronounced kah-MAHL-doe-lee) **Immaculate Heart Hermitage** was established in 1858 in a setting much like that of the original Order founded in the eleventh century by a monk named Romuald in the Appenines near Florence, Italy. Outsiders rarely see any of the twenty or so gentle, white-robed Camaldolese monks who are dedicated to a hermit-like way of life of prayer and creative and scholarly duties. The Hermitage has twenty-five cells for monks, a communal kitchen, a dining room, library, recreation room, nine rooms for guests on retreats, a small guest house, and cloistered quarters for women. Visitors are welcome to attend twice-daily Masses in the unadorned chapel. The anteroom is a little shop, run by volunteers, with religious artifacts and books, plus carvings and artworks made by the monks. Delicious brandied fruitcake is made in the Hermitage kitchen year-round and is sold here and at the Hermitage Shop in Carmel.

While Highway 1 was under construction, 163,000 cubic yards of rock had to be removed every thousand feet to curve the road under **Limekiln Point.** The bridge here spans a beautiful natural canyon with a waterfall. In the late 1800s schooners picked up bricks from Rockland Cement Company's four large kilns at the mouth of the creek. An easy half-mile walk will take you there. A short side trip off the same path leads to the waterfall. Jasper and iron pyrite can be found along this creek as can poor quality agates and garnets.

There are good campsites, trailer spaces, and a picnic area on bluffs overlooking the ocean at **Kirk Creek Campground,** operated by the U.S. Forest Service.

From the south end of Kirk Creek Bridge, **Nacimiento Grade** winds and climbs to nearly four thousand feet and then down to **Jolon** in the **San Antonio Valley,** about thirty miles. This is a narrow, asphalt-paved, scenic road. The highway leading out of Jolon goes to King City (twenty miles) on U.S. Highway 101. The Portolá expedition camped in San Antonio Valley in 1769, and in 1771 Padre Junipero Serra founded the third California Mission here, **San Antonio de Padua,** which eventually became one of the richest and most populous of the chain as hundreds of Indians were converted. At the outbreak of World War II, the Federal Government purchased thousands of acres of land adjacent to the Mission from William Randolph Hearst to establish **Hunter Liggett Military Reservation.** Hearst's holdings extended from his hunting lodge, now Hunter Liggett's headquarters, to fabled Hearst Castle at San Simeon to the south of Big Sur.

Pacific Valley is bordered by Wild Cattle Creek on the north and Prewitt Creek on the south. This is a four-mile stretch of rather level road, and access to the beach is easy for surf-anglers and skindivers.

By crossing the field beyond the parking lot at **Sand Dollar Picnic Area** and descending the stairs, you will reach a lovely, crescent-shaped beach. Watch for hang–gliders on the bluffs; they are here nearly every weekend enjoying coastal and mountain soaring.

The rugged Big Sur Coast

Just offshore you'll see a huge rock that, to early Spanish travelers, appeared to have rather feminine contours. They were the ones who gave the little town of **Gorda,** the last stop on the Big Sur mail run, its name. Gorda means "fat lady." After a rocky short-time existence under the ownership of Kidco Ltd. Ventures, a group of four teenagers from the San Diego area, who failed to meet their mortgage payments, this lively little ghost town is for sale again. About twelve people and a few dogs and cats live on the twenty- acre site; they work in the restaurant, store, or service station. A cluster of cabins appeared in the 1930s when the State began pushing the highway south to San Simeon, but the history of the area goes way back. The region took its place in the State's history in 1875 when the Los Burros Mining District was formed. The discovery of the coastal mother lode prompted the filing of over two thousand claims. However, Los Burros never really boomed, probably because of the difficulties in bringing ore out of the rugged terrain. Hundreds of thousands of dollars' worth of gold were taken out before the era ended. If Gorda is sold for the asking price of $950,000, it will be the biggest strike ever reported in the Los Burros District.

Plaskett Creek has another U.S. Forest Service campground with trailer and camping facilities, and about a quarter of a mile south, you can park and take the stairs down to Jade Cove's rocky beach.

Jade Cove has produced perhaps a million dollars' worth of quality nephrite jade in rare blue/green colors. Fine Pacific Blue Jade, found nowhere else in the world, is worth over $200 a pound. Prize specimens of this color are sought by collectors the world over. In 1971, a 9,000 pound hunk of nephrite jade, 8 1/2 feet long and 5 feet high, and worth $180,000, was dredged from beneath thirty feet of water near Jade Cove. *The Guinness Book of Records* lists it as the largest piece of jade ever found. Rockhounds have been busy here for many years, but it is still possible to find small pieces of jade on the beach and in the serpentine cliffs at this cove. Skindivers can bring up larger pieces. Most jade found nowadays is the common green and black serpentine and far from the real thing. The best specimens are found at low tide or after a winter storm. **Willow Creek** is an easy place to go down to the south end of Jade Cove where you can look for bits of jade stirred up by washing waves.

An easily overlooked dirt road leads to **Cape San Martin.** This is a good whale-watching spot, but the road is often impassable during winter months.

Just south of **Willow Creek Bridge** (562'), a narrow dirt road leads up to **Los Burros Mining District.** Mining roads are steep, rough, dusty, dry, and dangerous; a four-wheel drive vehicle is needed. The District stretches from Plaskett Ridge south of San Carpoforo Creek. Most of the land west of Hunter Liggett is open to prospecting and mining exploration, except private claims. Do not explore, prospect, hunt, or fish on land that may be inhabited. Mining claims may not be clearly marked, but trespassing is met sternly.

After leaving the mother lode in California's Gold Country, a few Chinese began exploring along the creeks in San Antonio Valley. They found a little gold, continued west, and eventually returned to their ancestral occupation, fishing. Around 1855 gold-bearing gravels were found in the westerly Santa Lucia Mountains, and many more miners moved in. Los Burros Mining District was formed by these miners in the 1870s. The District still produces small amounts of gold, silver, chromium, jade, and quicksilver. Every element known in the earth's crust and almost every geological condition is found in a small way somewhere in these high mountains. Even platinum has been found in the streams. A few present-day prospectors are seeking the legendary pot of gold; they work the old mines and skillfully recover tiny amounts of precious metals or hunt for large jade deposits near the coast.

Salmon Creek Waterfall is a few miles north of the Monterey County line and is in the southernmost stand of sequoia redwoods. Hardy hikers can clamber up the creek, climb behind the falls and get a damp, but delightful view through cascading water. This is an important steelhead trout spawning area. From the first heavy rains in the fall through January, steelhead spawn in most of the large creeks to the north.

Highway 1 winds southward to San Simeon and Hearst Castle, sixty-seven miles from the Big Sur Post Office. You have traveled through incomparable Big Sur country, and you will do so again because Big Sur always beckons. As Lillian Bos Ross mused, "Perhaps Big Sur is not a country at all, only a state of mind."

CHAPTER SEVEN

FOURISHING SEASIDE

Seaside owes its existence to Dr. John Lorenzo Dow Roberts, who came to the Monterey Peninsula in 1887 with only a brand new diploma from New York University's Medical School and a single silver dollar in his pocket. He bought a 160-acre ranch on what is now Seaside and Sand City from his uncle, David Houghton, for five thousand dollars on credit and filed a butcher paper map as his claim to the title. Within a year after subdividing the land, he had paid for it in full, had money in the bank, owned his own home, and had one thousand additional building lots to sell in what was then called "East Monterey." He founded the Post Office in 1890, and Seaside was born. He acted as Postmaster for forty-two years, and his wife later took on the duty.

Dr. Roberts became a familiar figure making house calls on horseback along the Big Sur coast, all the while charting the wilderness and dreaming of the day when there would be a highway. He saw that dream realized in 1937 when Highway 1 was dedicated.

When the steamer *Los Angeles* wrecked on the rocks off Point Sur, Dr. Roberts spent three days and nights helping to save the lives of 150 passengers.

In 1897, this remarkable man made a five-day trip on foot from San Luis Obispo to Monterey and mapped the rugged country in between. Eighteen years later he stood before the

Seaside residential area

California legislature showing colored slides on a bed sheet, and describing this magnificent area he loved so much. As a result, the State earmarked $1 $1/_2$ million for building another highway.

In the twenty years the doctor served on the Monterey County Board of Supervisors, four of them as Chairman, he never missed a meeting. He saw that the Presidio of Monterey, a former cow pasture, was enlarged and rebuilt in 1902 and pioneered the building of Highway 1 between Monterey and Castroville.

A fitting memorial to this outdoorsman of vision is **Roberts Lake** in Seaside where youngsters of all ages enjoy remote-control boating. It has been the site for international model boat racing competitions.

Seaside is bounded on the north and east by Fort Ord, Del Rey Oaks on the south, Monterey on the west, and Sand City and Monterey Bay on the northwest. The city's slogan is: "Seaside means business." It is the fastest growing residential and commercial community on the Monterey Peninsula with a population over forty thousand, five times its pre-World War II size.

The city has made great strides in overcoming its early image of a wide-open town of the new frontier. Seaside grew haphazardly until its incorporation in 1954. Speculators took their money and moved on, leaving the land little improved. Squatters built shacks and settled in the sand dunes and sagebrush and didn't bother to plant trees. During depression years lots sold for as little as one dollar. The *San Francisco Chronicle* offered free lots in Seaside as a come-on for new subscribers, few of whom ever settled here.

With the start of World War II and the establishment of the huge Fort Ord complex, land values rose. Since then an extensive urban renewal program has helped to replace substandard homes with hundreds of new homes in the growing residential areas overlooking the Peninsula's skyline and Mon-

Seaside City Hall, designed by Edward Durell Stone

terey Bay. Many military and civilian personnel from Fort Ord and the Naval Postgraduate School make their homes here. The citizens of Seaside are proud of their city's international character; nearly every country in the world is represented among its residents.

The **Seaside Chamber of Commerce,** 505 Broadway Avenue, is open 8:30 a.m.-5 p.m. Monday through Friday and welcomes your inquiries about the city and its many attractions.

Seaside City Hall, on a five and one-third acre site at 440 Harcourt Avenue, was designed by world-renowned architect Edward Durell Stone. A continuous and changing display of art works is on display here. Hours are 8 a.m.-5 p.m., closed Saturday and Sunday.

Oldemeyer Multi-Use Center, 986 Hilby Avenue, provides recreational and leisure activities for all ages. The complex has two major buildings; a twenty-six thousand square foot multi-purpose center, including an auditorium, youth and senior citizens' lounges, children's facilities, fine arts division, and meeting rooms, and a fourteen thousand square foot indoor swim center with a six-lane pool. The Center is open to the public from 8 a.m.-9 p.m. Monday through Friday with variable hours Saturday and Sunday. The pool is closed Sundays.

The **Monterey Peninsula Buddhist Temple,** 1155 Noche Buena, is an unexpected and appreciated sight. A latticed gate leads into a large compound of Oriental loveliness with its classic gardens, water falling into a pond full of koi, and to the glass-sided buildings beyond. English-speaking services are held Sundays at 10:15 a.m. First, second, and third generation Japanese (Isei, Nisei, and Sensei) sponsor a two-day Obon Festival at the Monterey County Fairgrounds in July and an Annual Bonsai Show at the Temple in May.

St. Seraphim's Russian Orthodox Church was built in the early 1950s on the site of Seaside's first Post Office, but has since been moved to Canyon Del Rey and Frances Avenue on the shores of Laguna Del Rey. It is worth driving by to see the church's Slavic architecture.

St. Seraphim's Russian Orthodox Church

Urban Redevelopment programs have made Seaside a forerunner of cities of its size. Among four renewal projects is the **Monterey Peninsula Auto Center,** a contemporary concept in new car shopping. It is a thirteen-dealer complex built around meandering pedestrian malls.

David Cutino Park (five acres) at Noche Buena and San Pablo Avenues has playground equipment, a full-sized athletic field, picnic area with barbecue pits, and a multi-use court for tennis, basketball, and volleyball.

An eight-foot wide, paved pedestrian-equestrian-bicycle trail starts at the northern edge of Seaside's city limits, running along the west side of the freeway, and goes to Fort Ord's main gate near Gigling Road where there is a vista point with a fine view of Monterey Bay. From there this $94,000 path leads all the way to Marina. This is the longest bike trail in the state and the first to be built next to a freeway.

CHAPTER EIGHT

CLOSE-BY COMMUNITIES

=======

DEL REY OAKS

In a sun pocket sandwiched between Monterey and Seaside, nestled in a grove of oak trees, is the quiet residential community of Del Rey Oaks. Since its incorporation in 1953, the two thousand residents have carefully preserved the family quality of Del Rey Oaks. All but four lots are zoned for single-family homes.

In the middle of the 286 wooded acres, on the floor of Canyon Del Rey, is a thirty-four acre park. The stream running through the canyon feeds Laguna Del Rey and Roberts Lake. Facilities include a recreation building, golf driving range, tennis courts, and a ball field, all built with aid from the Bing Crosby Youth Fund.

Tiny Pacific tree frogs (*Hyla regilla*) make their year-round home in the seventeen acre **Frog Pond Natural Area,** a part of the Monterey Peninsula Regional Park District in Del Rey Oaks. The area borders the north side of Canyon Del Rey Boulevard, between North-South Road in Fort Ord, and Carlton Drive. Parking is available at the City Hall and along the south side of Canyon Del Rey. Enter the Natural Area, which is open daily, through the willows at the junction of Via Verde. A sign marks the dirt pathway, a three-quarter mile loop that returns to the boardwalk. Brochures are available here for this self-guided nature trail. Bring your binoculars to view this interesting habitat for plants, birds, and animals. Wear comfortable walking shoes, and you might bring a change of socks and shoes during wet weather.

As you go along the wooden walkway over the frog pond, the little critters will probably shut up. Just wait a short while, and the chorus will begin again. Then you can follow the sound to their hiding places. These little tree frogs have chameleon qualities; they may be bright green or brown or somewhere in between, depending on their mood at the moment. You'll hear their mating songs in December and January. In the spring tadpoles line the pond's edge. As babies, Pacific tree frogs are vegetarians. Once they get their legs and establish their home on land, insects are preferred, with mosquitoes as their favorite entrée. There are other types of frogs and toads in the area, too.

Bird lovers will enjoy watching mallards and green teal ducks on the pond and hawks, chickadees, bushtits, and ruby-crowned kinglets in the wooded areas. Native wildflowers bloom in the spring, and there is a large stand of fragrant California roses.

Work Memorial Park, just west of the Frog Pond Natural Area, has picnic tables and a playground.

SAND CITY

Sand City is wedged between Seaside and Monterey Bay in the rolling dunes on the shoreside of the railroad tracks. It has the distinction of being the second smallest incorporated city in the state and is described as "a mile wide and a mile-and-a-half long." Sand City has a residential population of approximately five hundred, but nearly two thousand workers are employed in its commercial and light industrial establishments.

The only remaining fish cannery on the Monterey Peninsula is in Sand City. Monterey Fish Company operates about four months during the year, working whenever fishermen have brought in a catch the night before. Squid, mackerel, and anchovies are canned. These, plus cod and salmon, are also frozen and shipped all over the United States. Monterey Fish Company has a retail outlet on Municipal Wharf No. 2 in Monterey.

FORT ORD

Fort Ord was named after Maj. Gen. Edward Otho Cresap Ord, a nineteenth century famed Indian fighter who served as a Lieutenant under Gen. John C. Fremont, commanded the first U.S. Army garrison at the Presidio of Monterey, and distinguished himself as a combat officer in the Civil War.

In 1917 the Federal Government purchased 15,324 acres of sand dunes and scrub oaks near the present East Garrison for only $1.04 an acre. This land was known as Gigling Reservation, named after a German family who once lived in the area; Gigling Road still bears their name. At first the base, which consisted of a caretaker's house and a few bivouac sites, was used as a training ground for the old 11th Cavalry and 76th Artillery, both stationed at the Presidio. Then it remained dormant for many years except when National Guard and Army Reserve units trained in the summertime.

Twenty thousand acres were added in 1940, and Camp Ord became Fort Ord, a permanent Army base. The 7th Infantry was reactivated under the command of Gen. Joseph W. Stilwell and became the first major unit to occupy the post. During World War II years, Fort Ord was a staging and training area averaging about thirty-five thousand troops; at one time there were more than fifty thousand. The amphibians who made thirty invasions, including the reconquest of the Philippines, were trained here. Basic training was also provided for recruits for the Korean and Vietnam Wars.

Today Fort Ord covers 28,500 acres. Satellite operations include the 286,000 acre Hunter Liggett Military Reservation, seventy miles south, and 44,000 acre Camp Roberts, ninety miles south on Highway 101.

Once again the late "Vinegar Joe's" outfit has returned. Fort Ord has changed from its role as a basic training base to permanent brigade headquarters for the 7th Infantry. The reservation is home for nearly twenty-four thousand Army personnel and their families attached to four infantry battalions, a field artillery battalion, brigade headquarters, headquarters company, and selected support units. The 2nd Squadron of the 10th Air Cavalry has thirty helicopters assigned to reconnaissance and security, and the Army's Combat Development Experimentation Center, which tests new equipment and combat tactics, is also here.

An estimated 16,500 retired military from all branches of the armed services and their dependents use Fort Ord's facilities. Over two thousand civilians are employed here. Installations at the base include service clubs, libraries, theaters, craft shops, exchanges, indoor and outdoor sports facilities, chapels, and a 440-bed hospital that you can see on the skyline.

The 7th Infantry Division Museum is in Building 1040 near the intersection of First Avenue and First Street, one mile north of the Fort's main entrance next to Highway 1. Visitors can view historical displays spanning nearly a century of weapons, uniforms, equipment, documents, photographs, insignia, awards, and other memorabilia from the 7th Division's service in both World Wars and the Korean and Vietnam Wars. The museum is open to the public Monday-Thursday, 9 a.m.-12:30 p.m. and 1:30-4 p.m., including Federal holidays.

If you are curious about the red flags flying on the bayside of the highway, they indicate that the infantrymen are practicing on the target ranges.

Hang-gliding at Marina State Beach

MARINA

Sand from the dunes around present-day Marina was used as a primary source for rebuilding much of San Francisco following the disastrous 1906 earthquake and fire. Other than that, Sand Hill Ranch, as the area was known, produced only potatoes in those days. It was owned by David Jacks and James Bardin and later by John Armstrong.

With borrowed money, William Locke Paddon, a San Francisco land promoter with faith in the future, bought fifteen hundred acres of arid wasteland inhabited by rattlesnakes, ground squirrels, jack rabbits, and coyotes. Today there are many who wish they could have purchased property for $20 an acre in the heart of Marina as Paddon did in 1915. The little undeveloped land left in the Monterey Peninsula's third largest city now sells for hundreds of times that figure.

Paddon subdivided his desolate property into five-acre parcels and brought clients from San Francisco aboard the Southern Pacific for expense-paid weekends in "Paddonville," as the railroad company called it. The only greenery was in a sparse garden around the caretaker's old shack. Paddon was asking $75 an acre with $10 down, but buyers weren't too interested, so he was forced to sell on almost any terms, even $5 a month. The few who did settle were presented with cypress seedlings; some of the trees still form windbreaks on the dunes. The first residents, mostly French, eked out a living by growing potatoes, peas, turnips, and cabbages.

Not many people liked the name "Paddonville," so in 1919 with the establishment of a Post Office, it was changed to "Marina." Otherwise, the town changed little until after World War II when housing was needed for families of soldiers stationed at Fort Ord. The population doubled and redoubled several times. In the late 1950s subdivisions grew, and now there are acres of homes, hundreds of apartments, and several mobile home parks housing twenty-seven thousand residents. There are also six shopping areas and six schools. No longer a bedroom community for Fort Ord, incorporated in 1975, Marina is the "Gateway to the Monterey Peninsula."

Marina **Chamber of Commerce,** 3200 Del Monte Boulevard, is open from 9 a.m.- 4 p.m., Monday through Friday, and welcomes your inquiries.

Marina has a five-acre park on the knoll to the right of the highway on Del Monte Boulevard. Barbecue pits and picnic tables are available.

Marina State Beach (164 acres) is mostly undeveloped, but you can play in huge sand dunes or on the mile-long beach or do a little surf-fishing. It's too cold for sunbathing, and SWIMMING IS UNSAFE because of the strong undertow. A 1750' curving boardwalk for pedestrians and wheelchairs goes along the dunes, enabling you to view the natural area, a refuge for six rare endangered species: Menzies wallflowers, beach asters, Monterey Coast Indian paintbrush, coast gilia, Smith's blue butterflies, and black legless sand lizards. Parking for Marina State Beach is at the foot of Reservation Road. The park closes at sundown.

From the parking area, you can watch soaring hang-gliders. There is an almost constant northwest wind conducive to the sport. Enthusiasts can run down a sloping dune, take off, and not fall far if they miss.

A separated bicycle/pedestrian path on the west side of Del Monte Boulevard, between Reservation and Beach Roads, leads toward Castroville. Of course, you'll see acres and acres of globe artichokes (*Cynara scolymus*), the pride of Castroville, the "Artichoke Center of the World." Artichokes need these ideal growing conditions — rich, fast-draining soil, cool, foggy summers, and mild winters. A fifteen-mile radius of picturesque, precision-planted artichoke fields frames the town of Castroville.

CHAPTER NINE

HELPFUL SERVICES

(Area Code 408)

AIRCRAFT RENTALS

Avpak, 805 Airport Rd., Monterey, 372-7019

Del Monte Aviation, Inc., Monterey Peninsula Airport, Monterey, 373-4151

Jet Monterey, Monterey Peninsula Airport, Monterey, 375-7282

Kitty Hawk Kites, Reservations Rd. & Hwy. 1, Marina, 384-2622

Hang-gliding lessons - Monarch Aviation, Inc., Monterey Peninsula Airport Monterey, 373-3201

Monterey Peninsula Helicopters, Inc., 312 W. Carmel Valley Rd., Carmel Valley, 659-3898

SPI Helicopters, Monterey Peninsula Airport, Monterey, 372-1191

ART GALLERIES

The Monterey Peninsula abounds with art galleries. Check the Yellow Pages for a complete listing. The following are community-sponsored galleries:

Carmel Art Assn., Dolores & Sixth Ave., Carmel, 624-6176

Cherry Foundation, Guadalupe & Fourth Ave., Carmel 624-7491

Monterey History & Art Assn., 550 Calle Principal, Monterey, 372-2608

Monterey Peninsula Museum of Art, 559 Pacific St., Monterey, 372-7591

Pacific Grove Art Center, 568 Lighthouse Ave., Pacific Grove, 375-2208

Seaside City Hall Gallery, 440 Harcourt Ave., Seaside, 899-6208

Sunset Center, San Carlos & Ninth Ave., Carmel, 624-3996

ANTIQUE SHOPS

There are around seventy-five antique shops on the Monterey Peninsula. For a complete listing, consult the Yellow Pages.

AUTOMOBILE RENTALS

American Auto Rental, Inc., 801 Airport Rd., Monterey, 649-1611 or 649-0200

American International Rent-A-Car, 1000 Aguajito Rd., Monterey, 649-0240

Avis Rent A Car, Monterey Peninsula Airport, Monterey, 373-3327 and Ocean Ave. & Tenth, Carmel, 375-7050

Budget Rent A Car System, 2030 Fremont, Monterey, 373-1346

Dollar Rent-A-Car, Monterey Peninsula Airport, Monterey, 373-6121

Eagle Rent-A-Car, 2040 Del Monte Ave., Monterey, 646-1777

Freedom Rent-A-Car, 1178 Del Monte Ave., Monterey, 373-5178

Hertz Rent A Car, Monterey Peninsula Airport, Monterey, 373-3318

National Car Rental, Monterey Peninsula Airport, Monterey, 373-4181 or Doubletree Inn, Monterey, 373-2002

Sears Rent A Car, 2030 Fremont, Monterey, 373-1588

Ugly Duckling, 362 Reservation Rd., Marina, 384-9692

BED AND BREAKFAST INNS

A Place to Stay, Mission Ave., Carmel, 625-5136

Centrella Hotel, 612 Central Ave., Pacific Grove, 372-3372

The Cobblestone Inn, Junipero & Eighth Ave., Carmel, 625-5222

Country Cottages of Monterey, 1705 David Ave., Monterey, 375-5352

David Ave. Motor Court, 1705 David Ave., Monterey, 375-5352

Deet Jen's Big Sur Inn, Hwy. 1, Big Sur, 1-667-2377

Del Monte Beach Inn, 1110 Del Monte Ave., Monterey, 649-4410

Down Under Inn, 157 Fifteenth St., Pacific Grove, 373-2993

Gosby House Inn, 643 Lighthouse Ave., Pacific Grove, 375-1287

Green Gables Inn, 104 5th St., Pacific Grove, 375-2095

The Green Lantern Inn, Casanova & Seventh Ave., Carmel, 624-4392

Grosvenor's Garden Inn, Carpenter & Valley Way, Carmel, 624-3190

Happy Landing Inn, Monte Verde & Sixth Ave., Carmel, 624-7917

Hidden Valley Inn, 102 W. **Carmel Valley Rd.**, Carmel Valley, 659-5361

Holiday Guest House, Camino **Real & Seventh** Ave., Carmel, 624-6267

House of England, P.O. Box 223103, Carmel, 624-3004

The Jabberwock, 598 Laine, Monterey, 372-4777

Lincoln Green Inn, Dolores & Fourth Ave., Carmel, 624-1880

Maison Bleue, 157 Fifteenth St., Pacific Grove, 373-2993

Martine Bed & Breakfast Inn, 255 Ocean View Blvd., Pacific Grove, 373-3388

Merritt House, 386 Pacific St., Monterey, 646-9686

Monte Verde Inn, Monte Verde & Ocean Ave., Carmel, 624-6046

Normandy Inn, Ocean Ave. & Monte Verde, Carmel, 624-3825

Old Monterey Inn, 500 Martin, Monterey, 375-8284

The Old St. Angela Inn, 321 Central Ave., Pacific Grove, 372-3246

Pacific Gardens Inns, 701 Asilomar Ave., Pacific Grove, 646-9414

Pacific Grove Inn, Pine & Forest Aves., Pacific Grove, 375-2825

Roserox Country Inn by-the-sea, 557 Ocean View Blvd., Pacific Grove, 373-7673

San Antonio House, San Antonio & Ocean Aves., Carmel, 624-4334

Sandpiper Inn at-the-beach, 2408 Bay View Ave., Carmel, 624-6433

Sea View Inn, Camino Real & Eleventh Ave., Carmel, 624-8778

Seven Gables Inn, 555 Ocean View Blvd., Pacific Grove, 372-4341

Spindrift Inn, 652 Cannery Row, Monterey, 646-8900

The Stonehouse Inn, Eighth & Monte Verde Aves., Carmel, 624-4569

Vagabond's House, Dolores & Fourth Ave., Carmel, 624-7738

The Village Inn, Ocean Ave. & Junipero, Carmel, 624-3864

BICYCLE RENTALS

Bay Bikes, 640 Wave St., Monterey, 646-9090

Freewheeling Cycles, 188 Webster St., Monterey, 373-3855

Joselyn's Bicycles, 638 Lighthouse Ave., Monterey, 649-8520

W.M. & M. Cyclery, 214 Forest Ave., Pacific Grove, 372-2552

BOAT EXCURSIONS

Chris' Fishing Trips (375-5951), Randy's Fishing Trips (372-7440), and Sam's Fishing Fleet (372-0577), all on Fisherman's Wharf, Monterey, offer fishing and sightseeing tours year-round and whale-watching cruises during winter months.

Glass Bottom Belle, end of Fisherman's Wharf, Monterey, 372-7562. Motorpowered glass-bottom boat, operates 11 a.m - 6 p.m., holidays & weekends, daily in summer months.

Monterey Plaza Hotel Party Boat, Cannery Row, Monterey, 646-1700. Catered cruises for hotel guests and tour groups; sixty-foot catamaran accommodates forty-nine passengers.

Princess Monterey Cruises, 90 Fisherman's Wharf, Monterey, 372-2628

BOAT RENTALS

El Estero Boating, Lake El Estero, Monterey, 375-1484. Pedal boats & canoes for paddling around lake. Open daily 10:30 a.m.-5 p.m.

Kitty Hawk Sports, Reservation Rd. & Hwy. 1, Marina, 384-2622. Sailboards & windsurfing equipment.

Monterey Bay Yacht Center, Wharf No. 2, Monterey, 375-2002. Yacht rentals only.

BUS AND LIMOUSINE TOURS`

A-One Limousine Charter, Inc., 1425 Munras Ave., Monterey, 649-1425. Area tours; vans, buses, mini-buses, limousines.

Big Sur Getaway, Monterey-Salinas Transit Bus No. 22. Two round-trips daily from Monterey to Carmel/Big Sur during sum mer months, stopping at various locations along Hwy. 1, such as Carmel Highlands, Point Lobos, Bixby Creek Bridge, Pfeiffer Big Sur State Park, and Nepenthe. Limited service during winter months. Drivers have schedules, or call 899-2555.

California Heritage Guides, 10 Custom House Plaza, Monterey, 373-6454. Custom-designed motor tours using your car or theirs.

Gray Line of Monterey-Carmel, 373-4989. Bus tours of Monterey, Carmel, Pacific Grove, 17-Mile Drive, Carmel, and also to Hearst Castle (June-Sept.).

Joe's Taxi, Mission & Eighth Ave., Carmel, 624-3885. Guided scenic tours for small group.

Monterey-Salinas Transit, 1 Ryan Ranch Rd., Monterey, 899-2555. Routes extend throughout the Monterey Peninsula, serving many points of interest. System map at beginning of Yellow Pages. Complete riders' schedules and maps available from drivers. Exact fare 75¢ with transfer privileges; children four and under, free. Day pass for unlimited rides during one day, $2.00. Trips past Fort Ord or via Hwy. 68 (with access to Monterey Peninsula Airport) to Salinas leave every half hour from Monterey Transit Plaza, Tyler & Franklin Streets, Monterey. Free shuttle bus from downtown Monterey to points on Cannery Row and Monterey Bay Aquarium available every day during summer months and on weekends and holidays otherwise.

Seacoast Safaris, 1067 Sawmill Gulch Rd., Pebble Beach, 372-1288. Scenic tours of Monterey Peninsula, Big Sur, Hearst Castle, or Salinas Valley wineries; 14-passenger vans.

Steinbeck Country Tours Ltd., P.O. Box 22848, Carmel, 625-5107. Custom-designed chartered excursions and specialized trips throughout Steinbeck Country; 14-passenger vans; multilingual guides.

Tours of Distinction, 824 Munras Ave., Monterey, 373-0508. Specializing in custom-designed tours of convention groups; multi-lingual guides; 14-passenger vans, small and large buses.

USA Hosts-Monterey, 362 Pacific St., Monterey, 649-5115. Groups of ten or more; tours of Monterey Peninsula, Salinas Valley, or Hearst Castle; vans and buses.

Your Maitre D', P.O. Box 221696, Carmel, 624-1717. Complete entertainment program including gourmet dinners, catered parties, limousine tour service.

CHAMBERS OF COMMERCE

Carmel Business Assn., San Carlos & Seventh Ave., Carmel, 624-2522. Mon.-Fri., 9:30 a.m.-4 p.m.; Sat. during summer.

Carmel Valley Chamber of Commerce, 9 Delfino Pl., Carmel Valley, 659-4000. Tues., Wed., Thurs., 1-6 p.m.

Marina Chamber of Commerce, 3200 Del Monte Blvd., Marina, 384-9155. Mon.-Fri., 9 a.m.- 4 p.m.

Monterey Peninsula Chamber of Commerce, 380 Alvarado St., Monterey, 649-1770. Mon.-Fri., 8:30 a.m.-5 p.m.

Pacific Grove Chamber of Commerce, Forest & Central Aves., Pacific Grove, 373-3304. Mon.-Sat., 9 a.m.-5 p.m.

Seaside Chamber of Commerce, 505 Broadway Ave., Seaside, 394-6501. Mon.-Fri., 8:30 a.m.-5 p.m.

Visitors Information Center, YMCA, Webster & Camino El Estero, Monterey, 373-4166. Mon.-Fri., 8:30 a.m.-5:30 p.m.

FISHING TRIPS

All of the following provide daily fishing trips. Rates vary. Rods can be rented; bait is free with rental. Dress warmly and don't forget to pack a lunch and take along a thermos with a hot drink. Three-day fishing licenses are available on Fisherman's Wharf. If you plan to return to fish again, an annual license is a better buy. Youngsters under sixteen do not need licenses. Free licenses for persons over sixty-five are available from the Calif. State Dept. of Fish & Game, 2301 Garden Rd., Monterey, 639-1870.

Chris' Fishing Trips, 48 Fisherman's Wharf, Monterey, 375-5951

Monterey Bay Boat Works, 32 Cannery Row, Monterey, 373-7857

Randy's Fishing Trips, 66 Fisherman's Wharf, Monterey, 372-7440

Sam's Fishing Fleet, Inc. Fisherman's Wharf, Monterey, 372-0577

GOLF COURSES

Carmel Valley Golf & Country Club, Valley Greens Dr. & Carmel Valley Rd., Carmel Valley, 624-5323. 18 holes; private.

Carmel Valley Ranch Golf Course, 1 Old Ranch Rd., Carmel, 625-1010. 18 holes; private.

Cypress Point Golf Club, 17 Mile Dr., Pebble Beach, 624-6444. 18 holes; private.

Fort Ord Golf Course, 1300 Sylvan Rd., Monterey, 373-2436. 18 holes; public.

Laguna Seca Golf Club, York Rd., Monterey, 373-3701. 18 holes; public.

Monterey Peninsula Country Club, Del Monte Forest, Pebble Beach, 373-1556. Two 18-hole courses; private.

Naval Postgraduate School Golf Course, Fairgrounds & Garden Rds., Monterey, 646-2167. 18 holes; military.

Old Del Monte Golf Course, 1300 Sylvan Rd., Monterey, 373-2436. 18 holes; public.

Pacific Grove Municipal Golf Links, 77 Asilomar Ave., Pacific Grove, 373-3063. 18 holes; public.

Pebble Beach Golf Links, 17 Mile Dr., Pebble Beach, 624-3811. 18 holes; public.

Peter Hay Par 3 Golf Course, 17 Mile Dr., Pebble Beach, 624-3811. 9 holes; public.

Poppy Hills Golf Course, Lopez Rd., Pebble Beach, 625-2035. 18 holes; public.

Rancho Cañada Golf Club, Carmel Valley Rd., Carmel, 624-0111. Two 18-hole courses; public.

Spanish Bay Golf Links, 17 Mile Dr., Pebble Beach, 624-3811. 18 holes; public.

Spyglass Hill Golf Course, Spyglass Hill Rd. & Stevenson Dr., Pebble Beach, 624-3811. 18 holes; private.

HORSES FOR HIRE

Big Sur Trail Rides, Andrew Molera State Park, Big Sur, 1-625-8664

Pebble Beach Equestrian Center, Portola Rd., Pebble Beach, 624-2756. Reservations required; open daily.

Stonepine, 150 E. Carmel Valley Rd., Carmel Valley, 659-2245. Horsedrawn vehicles.

Ventana Wilderness Expeditions, Tassajara Rd., Carmel Valley, 659-0433

MUSEUMS

Allen Knight Maritime Museum, Custom House Plaza, Monterey, 375-2553. Weekdays, 1-4 p.m.; Sat. and Sun., 2-4 p.m.; closed holidays.

Bear Flag Museum, Eureka Federal Savings & Loan Assn., 599 Lighthouse Ave., Pacific Grove, 646-8222. Mon.-Fri., 8 a.m.- 5 p.m.; free.

Carmel Mission Basilica (2 museums) Rio Rd., Carmel, 624-1271. Weekdays, 9:30 a.m.-5 p.m.; Sun., 10:30 a.m.-5 p.m.; voluntary contribution.

Colton Hall Museum, Pacific at Jefferson, Monterey, 375-9944. Daily 10 a.m.-noon & 1-4 p.m.; until 5 p.m. spring and summer; free.

Ford Ord 7th Infantry Division Museum, Building 1040, Fort Ord, 242-3804. Thurs.-Mon. 9 a.m.-12:30 p.m. & 1:30-4 p.m.; free.

Monterey Peninsula Museum of Art, 599 Pacific St., Monterey, 372-7591. Tues.-Sat. 10 a.m.-4 p.m.; Sun. 1-4 p.m.; free.

Pacific Grove Heritage Society, Ketchum's Barn, Seventeenth St. & Laurel Ave., Pacific Grove. Sat. 1-4 p.m. year-round; Wed., Thurs., & Fri. noon-4 p.m., May thru Sept. ; free.

Pacific Grove Museum of Natural History, 165 Forest Ave., Pacific Grove, 372-4212. 10 a.m.-4 p.m.; closed Mon. ; free.

Point Pinos Light Station Museum, Ocean View Blvd., Pacific Grove, 375-2278. Sat. & Sun. 1-4 p.m.; free.

Spirit of Monterey Wax Museum, 700 Cannery Row, Monterey, 375-3770. Daily 9 a.m.-9 p.m. in summertime; 10 a.m.-7 p.m wintertime; adults $3.95; children twelve & under accompanied by adult, free; children under twelve alone $1.25.

U.S. Army Museum, Presidio, Monterey, 647-5184. Mon.-Fri. 9-11:45 a.m. & 12:30-4 p.m.; closed holidays; free.

RECREATIONAL VEHICLE AND CAMPING FACILITIES

BIG SUR

Big Sur Campgrounds & Cabins, Hwy. 1, Big Sur 1-667-2322

Fernwood, Hwy. 1, Big Sur, 1-667-2422

Limekiln Beach Redwoods, Big Sur, 1-667-2403

Pfeiffer Big Sur State Park, Big Sur, 1-667-2423

Riverside Campgrounds & Cabins, Big Sur, 1-667-2414

Ventana Campgrounds, Big Sur, 1-667-2331 or 624-4812

The U.S. Forest Service has several campgrounds south of Big Sur village. Information can be obtained at the Big Sur Guard Station just south of the entrance to Pfeiffer Big Sur State Park.

CARMEL VALLEY

Riverside RV Park, Schulte Rd., Carmel Valley, 624-9329

Saddle Mountain Recreation Park, Schulte Rd., Carmel Valley, 624-1617

Information about campgrounds in Los Padres National Forest is available at the Ranger Station at Los Padres Dam.

MARINA

Marina Dunes RV Park, 3330 Dunes Dr., Marina, 384-6914

MONTEREY

Laguna Seca Recreation Area, 1025 Monterey Rd., Salinas, 1-422-6138

Veterans Memorial Park (municipal), Jefferson St. & Skyline Dr., Monterey, 646-3865

SHOPPING AREAS

American Tin Cannery, 125 Ocean View Blvd., Pacific Grove

The Barnyard, Mouth of Carmel Valley, Carmel

Carmel Rancho Square, Mouth of Carmel Valley, Carmel

Cannery Row Shops, Cannery Row, Monterey

Carmel Center, Mouth of Carmel Valley, Carmel

Carmel Plaza, Ocean Ave., Carmel

Carmel Stores, Vicinity Ocean Ave., Carmel

Carmel Valley Stores, Carmel Valley Rd., Carmel Valley

Country Club Gate Center, Forest & David Aves., Pacific Grove

The Crossroads, Mouth of Carmel Valley, Carmel

Del Monte Shopping Center, Hwy. 1 & Munras Ave., Monterey

Doubletree Mall, Alvarado St., Monterey

Fairway Shopping Center, Forest Ave., Pacific Grove

Fisherman's Wharf Shops, Fisherman's Wharf, Monterey

Marina Stores, Vicinity Reservation Rd., Marina

Mid-Valley Shopping Center, 312 W. Carmel Valley Rd., Carmel Valley

Monte Vista Village, Soledad Dr., Monterey

Monterey Stores, Vicinity Alvarado St., Monterey

New Monterey Stores, Vicinity Lighthouse Ave., Monterey

Olympia Plaza, 1760 Fremont Blvd., Seaside

Pacific Grove Stores, Vicinity Lighthouse Ave., Pacific Grove

Pebble Beach Shops, 17 Mile Dr., Pebble Beach

Seaside Stores, Vicinity Broadway Ave., Fremont Blvd. & Del Monte Blvd., Seaside

Valley Hills Shopping Center, Carmel Valley Rd., Carmel Valley

SKINDIVING AND SCUBA EQUIPMENT RENTALS

Aquarius Dive Shop, 2240 Del Monte Ave., Monterey, 375-1933 and 32 Cannery Row, Monterey, 375-6605

Bamboo Reef Enterprises, Inc., 614 Lighthouse., Monterey, 372-1685

Monterey Bay Wetsuits, 121-D Ocean View Blvd., Pacific Grove, 375-7848

SWIMMING FACILITIES

Carmel Valley Community Pool, Ford & Carmel Valley Rds., Carmel Valley, 659-2606. Public

Carmel Valley Racquet Club, 27300 Rancho San Carlos Rd., Carmel, 624-2737. Private

Children's Pool, Lovers Point, Pacific Grove, 372-2802. Public.

Los Laureles Lodge, Carmel Valley Rd. & Rancho Rd., Carmel Valley, 659-2233. Public; adults only.

Meadowbrook Swim & Tennis Club, 1553 Kimball Ave., Seaside, 394-6629. Private.

Pattulo Swim Center, 1184 Wheeler, Seaside, 899-6270. Public.

Saddle Mountain Recreation Park, Schulte Rd., Carmel Valley, 624-1617. Public.

Tawse Pool, Dennis the Menace Park, Monterey. Public.

TENNIS FACILITIES

Carmel Valley Inn & Tennis Resort, Carmel Valley Rd. & Los Laureles Rd., Carmel Valley, 659-3131. Public

Carmel Valley Racquet Club, 27300 Rancho San Carlos Rd., Carmel, 624-2737. Private.

Carmel Valley Ranch Tennis Club, 1 Old Ranch Rd., Carmel, 635-0922. Private.

Hyatt Regency Monterey Racquet Club, 1 Old Golf Course Rd., Monterey, 372-1234. Public.

John Gardiner's Tennis Ranch, Carmel Valley Rd., Carmel Valley, 659-2207. Private.

Meadowbrook Swim & Tennis Club, 1553 Kimball Ave., Seaside, 394-6629. Private.

Mission Tennis Ranch, 26260 Dolores, Carmel, 624-4335. Public.

Monterey Tennis Center, 401 Pearl St., Monterey, 372-0172. Public.

Pacific Grove Tennis Center, 515 Junipero Ave., Pacific Grove, 372-2809. Public.

WALKING TOURS

California Heritage Guides provide an enjoyable way to explore Monterey. Four walking tours, conducted by qualified guides, are offered nearly every day year-round: Tour No. 1, Robert Louis Stevenson House area; Tour No. 2, Custom House Plaza area; Tour No. 3, Monterey Town House and Old Jail area; and Tour No. 4, Cannery Row. The average tour lasts 1 1/2-2 hours. Admission fees per tour are inexpensive and include entrance fees to historic buildings where required. Call 373-6454 for necessary reser-

vations. California Heritage Guides office, 10 Custom
House Plaza, Monterey, is open 10 a.m.-5 p.m. in summertime & 10 a.m.-4 p.m. in winter.

Gallery Tour of Carmel-by-the-Sea is a free guide, including
a good map of the village and is available at all Carmel
galleries and from major hotels, motels, and restaurants in
Carmel.

Path of History is Monterey's well-marked, self-guided, 2.7
mile tour of forty-six historic buildings, including Custom
House, Colton Hall, Robert Louis Stevenson House,
California's First Theatre, Old Whaling Station, and other
sites rich in the area's history. Some have curators on duty
and are open to the public; others are private offices and
homes. A few of the historic buildings require small entrance fees. Free maps are available at the Monterey History
& Art Assn., 550 Calle Principal, Monterey, and at the
Monterey Peninsula Chamber of Commerce, 380 Alvarado
St., Monterey. Follow the big blue dots on Monterey's
downtown sidewalks.

WINERIES

Bargetto Winery of Cannery Row, 702 Cannery Row, Monterey, 373-4053

Chateau Julien Winery, 8940 Carmel Valley Rd., Carmel
Valley, 624-2600

Durney Vineyard, Cachagua Rd., Carmel Valley, 625-5433

Monterey Peninsula Winery, 786 Wave St., Monterey,
372-4949 and 467 Shasta Ave., Sand City, 394-2999

Smith & Hook Winery, 217 Crossroads Blvd., Carmel,
625-6480

Robert Talbott Vineyard, Tassajara Rd., Carmel Valley, 659-5522

Ventana Vineyards Tasting Room, 2999 Monterey-Salinas, Monterey, 372-7415

YOUTH HOSTEL

Check with the YMCA of the Monterey Peninsula, 600 Camino El Estero, Monterey, 373-4167. Summer months only; sites vary.

CHAPTER TEN

CALENDAR OF ANNUAL EVENTS

Information concerning all of these events is available from the various Chambers of Commerce on the Monterey Peninsula.

JANUARY

Pebble Beach National Pro-Am Golf Championship, various courses, 1 week

Spalding Invitational Pro-Am Golf Tournament, various courses, 1 week

FEBRUARY

Dixieland Monterey, downtown Monterey clubs, 3 days

Hot Air Balloon Races, Laguna Seca Recreation Area, 3 days

Monterey Film Festival, various theatres, 4 days

Mushroom Show, Pacific Grove Museum of Natural History, 2 days

Pacific Grove City Open Golf Tournament, Pacific Grove Municipal Golf Links, 2 days

MARCH

Hang Glider Steeplechase, Marina State Beach, 2 days

Kite Festival, Carmel High School

Monterey National Invitational Rugby Tournament, Collins Field, Pebble Beach

Monterey Peninsula Open Golf Championship, Old Del Monte Golf Course, Monterey, 2 days

Monterey Wine Festival, Monterey Conference Center, 4 days

Science Fair, Monterey Fairgrounds, 3 days

UCSTA Combined Equestrian Tests, Equestrian Center, Pebble Beach

APRIL

Adobe Tour, downtown Monterey

Comicon (comic book convention), Monterey Conference Center

Easter Egg Hunt, Caledonia Park, Pacific Grove

Easter Egg Hunt, El Estero Ball Park, Monterey

Good Old Days, Pacific Grove, 1 week

High School Jazz Competition, Monterey Fairgrounds

International Marathon, Big Sur to Carmel

Monterey Bay Hang Gliding Steeple Chase, Marina State Beach, 3 days

Quilt Show, Chautauqua Hall, Pacific Grove, 2 days

Victorian House Tour, Pacific Grove

Wildflower Show, Pacific Grove Museum of Natural History, 3 days

MAY

Bocci Ball Tournament, Custom House Plaza, Monterey

California State Fish & Game Mariculture Laboratory

Open House, Granite Canyon, Big Sur

Del Monte Kennel Club Dog Show, The Lodge at Pebble Beach

Great Monterey Squid Festival, Monterey Fairgrounds, 2 days

IMSA Camel GT Auto Races, Laguna Seca Raceway, Monterey
Concours, Monterey Fairgrounds

Language Day Open House, Presidio, Monterey

Monterey Rugby Classic, Collins Field, Pebble Beach, 2 days

Monterey Triple Crown, Laguna Seca Raceway, 2 days

NCGA Two Man Golf Championship, Spyglass Hill Golf
Course, Pebble beach, 3 days

Tor House Foundation Garden Party, Tor House, Carmel

Wildflower Show, Tularcitos School, Carmel Valley, 2 days

JUNE

Fiesta de los Padres, San Carlos Cathedral, Monterey

Merienda, Memory Garden, Monterey

Monterey Bay Blues Festival, Monterey Fairgrounds, 2 days

Monterey Summer Sprints, Laguna Seca Raceway, 2 days

Otter Regatta, Monterey Bay, 2 days

Swallows Golf Tournament, Pebble Beach courses, 4 days

JULY

American Heritage Week, Fort Ord

Arabian Horse Show, Monterey Fairgrounds, 3 days

Camel Pro National Championships, Laguna Seca Raceway, 2
days

Carmel Bach Festival, Sunset Center & Carmel Mission Basilica,
2 weeks

Champion 200 Motorcycle Races, Laguna Seca Raceway, 3 days

Feast of Lanterns, Pacific Grove, 4 days

Festival of the Holy Spirit, San Carlos Cathedral, Monterey, 2 days

Fleet Week, Monterey Bay

Fourth of July Parade, Seaside

Jenkins Regatta, Stillwater Cove, Pebble Beach, 2 days

Monterey Multihill Classic, Monterey Bay, 6 days

Morgan Horse Show, Monterey Fairgrounds, 3 days

National Horse Show, Monterey Fairgrounds, 3 days

Obon Festival, Monterey Fairgrounds, 2 days

Scottish Highland Games, Monterey Peninsula College, Monterey

Sloat Landing Celebration, Presidio & Custom House Plaza, Monterey

Western Days, Marina, 1 week

AUGUST

Concours d'Élégance, The Lodge at Pebble Beach

Culturama, Laguna Seca Recreation Area, 2 days

Flight of the Monarch Golf Tournament, Pacific Grove Municipal Golf Links

Historic Automobile Races, Laguna Seca Raceway, 3 days

Jenkins Championship Series, Stillwater Cove, Pebble Beach

Monterey Bay TheatreFest, Monterey, 2 days

Monterey County Fair, Monterey Fairgrounds, 6 days

Monterey Square Dance Festival, Seaside High School, 3 days

NCGA Amateur Match Play, Spyglass Hill Golf Course, Pebble Beach, 6 days

NCGA Public Links Championship, 2 days
Our Lady of Fatima Parade, Pacific Grove
Pebble Beach Summer Horse Show, Equestrian Center, 6 days

SEPTEMBER

California Challenge Polo Match, Collins Field, Pebble Beach
Fiesta de San Carlos Borromeo, Carmel Mission Basilica
Labor Day Regatta, Stillwater Cove, Pebble Beach
Monarch Golf Tournament, Pacific Grove Municipal Golf Links
Monterey Jazz Festival, Monterey Fairgrounds, 3 days
Parade of Nations International Festival, Custom House Plaza, Monterey, 2 days
Peruvian Horse Show, Monterey Fairgrounds, 3 days
Plaza Cup Regatta, Monterey Bay
Run for the Beacon, Pacific Grove
Santa Rosalia Festival, Custom House Plaza, Monterey
Seaside-Sand City Bazaar and Bed Races, Seaside

OCTOBER

Big Sur River Run, Big Sur
Butterflies and Breakers 10K Run, Pacific Grove
Butterfly Parade and Bazaar, Pacific Grove
Carmel Valley Rodeo, Carmel Valley Trail and Saddle Club, 2 days
Chili Feed and Crafts Fair, Custom House Plaza, Monterey
Great Sand Castle Contest, Carmel Beach
Little Children's Autumn Festival, Laguna Seca Recreation Area

Monterey Grand Prix, Laguna Seca Raceway, 2 days

NCGA Two-Man Net Championships, Spyglass Hill, Pebble beach

Oktoberfest, Laguna Seca Recreation Area, 2 days

Parade of Champions, Seaside

Pumpkin Carving Contest, The Barnyard, Carmel

Pro Celebrity Tennis Tournament, Hyatt Regency, Monterey, 3 days

Tor House Festival, Carmel 2 days

Week of the Bayonet, Fort Ord

1930 Packard at the Concours d'Élégance

NOVEMBER

Catamaran Regatta, Monterey Bay, 2 days

Championship High School Marching Band Festival, Pacific Grove High School

Classic Guitar Festival, Sunset Center, Carmel, 3 days

Community Thanksgiving Dinner, Monterey Fairgrounds

Robert Louis Stevenson Un-Birthday, Stevenson House, Monterey

DECEMBER

California Women's Amateur Golf Championship, Pebble Beach, 6 days

Christmas at the Inns, Pacific Grove

Christmas in the Adobes, downtown Monterey, 2 days

Community Christmas Dinner, Monterey Fairgrounds

East of Eden Cat Fanciers Show, Monterey Fairgrounds

European Christmas Market, The Barnyard, Carmel

Festival of the Trees, Monterey Fairgrounds, 4 days

Posada Procession and Piñata Party, Monterey Conference Center

Singing Christmas Tree, Cannery Row, Monterey

About the Authors

A transplanted Washingtonian, Maxine Knox, since moving with her husband and sons to the Monterey Peninsula thirty years ago, has done advertising and business promotion for hotels and restaurants. She and her husband live in Pacific Grove.

As the wife of a Navy Commander, Mary Rodriguez and her daughters lived in many places, but on her husband's retirement Monterey became their permanent home, also thirty years ago. Mary is a staff writer for *This Month Magazine*.

A mutual hobby, contesting, at which they are successful, brought Maxine and Mary together and their friendship grew into a writing team, at which they are equally successful. This book is their fifth team effort.

INDEX

H

I

J

Y

Z